Mysteries of Life

Questions Answered

&

Symbols and their Meaning

Joyce Welch

FANTINE PRESS

Published by
Fantine Press
The Coach House
Stansted Hall
Stansted
Essex CM24 8UD

ISBN 1 901958 08 6

Printed in England by Booksprint

FOREWORD

THE contents of this book, the result of years of painstaking work and constant communication with her spirit teachers, have been brought to us by a very dedicated and spiritual lady whose only wish is to help others in any way that she can. Her selfless work in spiritual guidance and teaching has helped many, many people already. It is her hope that she can reach and help many more - those who are not in a position to meet her face to face. At all times she is endeavouring to bring to everyone an understanding of the great love and simplicity of Spirit.

Ann Ward

ACKNOWLEDGEMENT

THANK YOU isn't enough to my dear loyal friend Ann Ward. Having you as a friend is one of the best things that has ever happened to me. Loyal friends are like diamonds – you don't find them on the ground ready to be picked up, but you can find them when you're in the dark times of your life, in the "pits" of your misery, and that's when I discovered you were one of my most loyal friends.

Without Spirit I know this book would not have been possible. Their teachings, wisdom and enlightenment have been the reason why this book of questions and answers has been written. In fact, they are the true authors of 'Mysteries of Life.'

Ann, you were such a great help. You spent your summer, autumn and winter of 2003 working with me. You sat at your computer, at times in great pain, and yet I never once heard you complain. There were times when I could see that a word would seem wrong in a sentence, or did not fit in, and I would ask Spirit for confirmation. Back you would go to your computer, happy to be of service. I so value your friendship, your sense of humour, and your sincerity. You have proved to be an excellent teacher. I always thought you would, because the moment you came into my class, your willingness to learn and explore showed me your commitment to serve Spirit and mankind.

I also wish to express my sincere thanks to Tony Ward for his contributions. You deserve a medal for putting up with Ann and Yours Truly! Why must women always be right, Tony?

A belated, but nevertheless sincere Thank You to Yvonne Bailey for the help you gave so freely with my first book.

Also thanks to my illustrators, Louise Stevenson and Dafydd Davies.

Thank you, friends.

CONTENTS

INTRODUCTION

THROUGHOUT the ages spiritual masters have come to this planet to bring teachings and guidance from the Spirit World. These teachings have given rise to much discussion and strife, and will no doubt continue to do so in the foreseeable future. Despite the basic premise of these spiritual teachings being love and tolerance, mankind has always placed his own interpretation upon them. They have been used to further dynastic aspirations, political ends and the wish for power and material gain.

The teachings given in the past have been appropriate for the level of mankind's understanding at that particular time in history. Now we are in the age of Aquarius, the age of the mind when people are questioning, thinking for themselves, not in need of dogmas and fixed ideas which have held back the spiritual development of so many people, the age when people do not want all aspects of their faith dictated to them by others.

Now we wish to know answers to basic questions, like where have we come from, why are we here and what should we be doing about it while we are here in a physical body on this particular planet and, most importantly, do we in some form or other, live on after our physical death to eternally rest in peace or is there the possibility of an even more exciting future for us all?

Because religions have always put an intermediary – rabbi, priest, imam, guru, vicar etc. between us and the Spirit World, we have forgotten that it is perfectly natural, not mystical, for us to communicate directly with the Spirit World.

Are we really able to communicate with the Spirit World or is it a case of 'out of sight, out of mind'? Not at all. The Spirit

World is a world of love, and the occupants thereof wish to continue helping us. After all, they have experienced life on a planet and know how much we need guidance and upliftment.

To further this aim, our primary contact with the Spirit World is our guardian angel who is always communicating with us, trying to impress us to follow the right spiritual pathway.

There is nothing new in the teachings set out in this book; they have always existed in the same form and always will. They do not need to change with the times or the fashions of the moment. It is our appreciation of the teachings that needs to change. These teachings are a perfect blend of logic, justice and spirituality and apply to everyone. They are truly universal, for wherever there is life in our universe, they apply in exactly the same way. Certainly at times we do not appreciate their significance to us as individuals, but upon our return to the Spirit World we will recognise that it is so.

In an attempt to enlighten the reader the first part of this book consists of a series of questions and answers, which provide thought provoking subjects for consideration and discussion.

What if, after due consideration, we feel unable to accept the answers? Then we must set them aside, leave them on the shelf. However, it is surprising how many times, after talking to someone about their experiences, having read something, or going through a major experience in our life, we are then able to see the relevance of an answer. Whatever else we are not convinced about, dismissing the ideas of love and tolerance is something we do at our peril.

But there are many questions that remain unanswered because when we have asked them of our spiritual helpers, they have explained that the level of our understanding while in a physical body is reduced to such an extent that we could not possibly comprehend the answers. There are also details that have not been expanded upon for the same reasons. Therefore you will find from time to time in the book, references to that fact that we will not understand certain things until we return to the Spirit World.

The second part of the book shows another way in which understanding is brought to us. The universal language used by the Spirit World is symbolic in communication. Whereas in oral communication we have to use different languages for different races, the language of symbols can be used to communicate with anyone; the picture of a bicycle, a flower or a bird has the same meaning for everyone, no matter the spoken language or nationality.

Dreams are another method by which the Spirit World communicates with us, and once more the language of symbols comes into its own. But how are you going to be able to interpret the meaning of these symbols? This is where the second part of this book will be able to assist, as we have given you a dictionary of symbols from which you can work. It would be impossible to include every word that may be used but you will find that as your awareness develops your ability to break down symbols and communicate with Spirit will improve.

The author's hope is that the information contained in this book will enable readers to add to their self awareness, their own spirituality and their understanding of others, also to tap the help and guidance freely offered by those in the Spirit World. Furtherance of these aims can only help in mankind's struggle to bring true peace of mind and prosperity to all living on our beautiful planet.

Questions and Answers on the Spirit

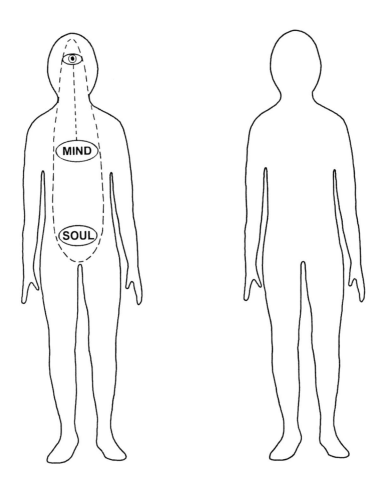

The shape representing the spirit is only symbolic as we do not know what it really looks like.

What is the spirit and what effect can we see from its existence?
It is strange how people in this world know that there is a wind, and they are quite happy to know and accept it, even though it cannot be seen. They do not question this. The same applies to the air that we breathe, and again nobody questions its existence. An electric current is invisible too, but of course we know it exists. Each of these have an effect that we *can* see, and so too does the spirit, even though dissecting the physical body will not reveal it because it is not of physical matter as we know it.

We are spirit encased in a physical, human body, and the effect from the spirit is life itself. Without a spirit the body is dead – a corpse. Our natural state is pure spirit and while we are in the physical body we are in an unnatural state – imprisoned until physical death.

Why is the word 'soul' used when referring to a person instead of the word 'spirit?'
The word 'soul' has been used instead of the word 'spirit' for a number of years. It is a matter of preference but is inaccurate as the soul is *part* of the spirit. It may have come about from the reference to someone as being a kind soul or a hard soul because this is referring to the emotions describing the person, and the soul is the source of all emotions.

Why do we come onto a physical planet?
The physical planet has been designed for the purpose of supporting physical life because living a physical life gives us experiences outside those we would encounter in the Spirit World. Whilst we are living and working on a planet, we need a physical body to carry out physical tasks. But we also have obstacles to overcome which are associated with physical life and having a physical body. Being in a physical body we have to understand basic survival lessons, such as the need to eat, to find shelter and procreate.

In addition to this, we experience negative emotions such as hatred, bitterness and jealousy that do not exist in that world of love that is the Spirit World. We have temptations to overcome and we have to learn how to survive in a material world, yet resist the lure of becoming greedy and materialistic.

We need to learn how to co-exist with those of a different culture, colour, intelligence, and even those whose opinions are directly opposed to our own. In so doing, we learn tolerance and understanding.

We are here to learn lessons and grow spiritually; the planet is a school of learning for us. Here we have the opportunity to evolve, to expand the mind with wisdom and the soul with kindness, compassion and love. But it is a difficult project, and all the more rewarding when we achieve our objectives.

When does the spirit body enter the physical body?
At conception.

How does it get there?
It is placed there by Spirit. How this is accomplished we could not begin to understand! We only know that quite a lot of preparation is necessary before the process can take place.

In the case of identical twins, at what point does the spirit enter the womb?
There will be two spirits, and they are not placed in the womb until the fertilised egg has split into two. Even though they are identical in the physical sense they are not necessarily so in spirituality. They are individual spirits and as such follow their own spiritual pathway, which could differ enormously according to how evolved they are. They do not necessarily come from the same spirit family (see Spirit Groups).

Do parents of a new baby play a part in the creation of the baby's spirit?
The spirit has always existed. It comes from the Spirit World

to be housed in a physical body. It takes a male and a female to create the physical body, but they cannot create the spirit. That is something that only the God power can do.

The God power is the creator of all life and there cannot be life in a body unless the spirit is within.

What does the spirit body consist of?
The two main components are the mind and the soul.

What is their function?
The mind is the source of all our thoughts, and the soul is the seat of all our emotions.

Whilst the spirit is in a physical body, the mind works through the brain so that our thoughts can be put into action, and our five senses utilised. The soul brings with it from the Spirit World the sum of the love and compassion we have accumulated through our spiritual growth in previous lives. The choice of how much or little we express of this love is up to us.

Do the components of the spirit body function independently of one another?
No. We cannot have a thought without a feeling about it, and we cannot have a feeling without a thought. For instance, we suddenly remember that tomorrow we have an important interview to attend and immediately our soul responds by feeling nervous, affecting the organs in the physical body in close proximity to it. We feel butterflies in the stomach etc.

Where does the spirit body lie in relation to the physical body?
In the torso. The mind is situated in the area of the chest just above the heart, and sometimes when Spirit draws close thus stimulating the mind, it can seem like a slight form of palpitation. The soul is located in the abdominal region, and because of its close proximity to the stomach, bladder and bowel, emotional upsets can adversely affect these organs e.g. butterflies in the stomach and upsets in the abdominal area.

What attaches the spirit body to the physical body?
A silver cord attaches the spirit body to the physical body and is situated at the base of the spine, performing a similar function as the umbilical cord with the baby in the womb. The umbilical cord is cut at the birth of the physical body, and the silver cord is cut at the death of the physical body.

The silver cord is not of the physical but of the spirit, and thus cannot be seen by the physical eye.

When the time finally arrives for the spirit to return to the Spirit World, when the allotted time has been reached or the physical body cannot sustain life any more, the silver cord is cut by our guardian angel. Only then does life leave the physical body. The spirit is released from its material 'prison' and cannot return there. How the cord is cut we do not know. As with many occurrences linked with the Spirit World, we will only understand once our mind is unlocked.

We cannot remember anything of our life before coming onto the earth. Why is this?
The part of our spirit which retains all our memories of life in the Spirit World – the mind – is locked, and remains so until we return to the Spirit World.

Whilst we are on the planet in a physical body our primary need is to concentrate on our life here. If we were allowed to remember all our previous lives and the love and tranquillity of the Spirit World, we would not want to stay on the planet a moment longer than necessary, and could be extremely unhappy and confused, unable to settle down. Our one wish would be to return to our spirit home.

What support do we get from the Spirit World?
Firstly, of course, we have our guardian angel, who is there beside us from conception to death, guiding us along our spiritual pathway.

Secondly, those of our loved ones who have passed over to the Spirit World will also be beside us in our times of need.

When there is sadness and suffering within our physical family they are close at hand, giving us all the love, comfort and support that they would have given had they been with us in the physical world, but the wisdom and compassion that is now there is so much greater.

Lastly, there are others from the Spirit World who, unlike our guardian angel, are there at specific times. They will help us in the areas in which they have expertise e.g. spiritual healing, science and technology. They come from varied walks of life in the physical world and are interested in, and wish to give support and inspiration to those who are following in their footsteps.

Many a good doctor or surgeon will have a spirit helper who was in the same field of medicine, and who now draws close to advise them in ministering to their patients. Scientists too can have a spirit helper with them in the laboratory when they are working and many of their ideas have been planted in their minds by spirit helpers. Many composers, musicians and great leaders have unknowingly been helped by those from the Spirit World.

When does our guardian angel join forces with us?
Once it is agreed that we will be allowed to come to this planet, there will be a meeting to decide who will be our guardian angel. It will always be someone whom we know from our time in the Spirit World, and who will be from our spirit family. Those who are involved in placing the spirit in the physical body will ensure that our guardian angel is there at conception, ready to take on their responsibilities, remaining at our side from that time onwards.

If our guardian angel is with us all the time, do they intrude on our private moments?
It is not easy for us to understand the relationship between our guardian angel and ourselves and how it works. It is not the same as having our every move recorded; it is more

of a mind-to-mind communication. Our need for privacy is respected at all times, and our guardian angels, figuratively speaking, turn their backs to us at our very private moments.

How do our guardian angel and other spirit helpers communicate with us?

Throughout our lives we have been impressed and inspired by our guardian angel and other spirit helpers. Through our lack of understanding, we are not aware of this but they are able to come close to us to work mind-to-mind. Perhaps the only time when we may recognise their input is when we surprise ourselves with something we say or do.

During sleep they communicate with us in the form of dreams. Quite often we do not get the message because we do not understand the symbolic meanings contained in the dreams, but the message is there nevertheless. Or they may engineer a meeting during our sleep state to help or advise us. It is unlikely that we will remember it, but it will be filed in the future subconscious part of our mind for future reference.

Communication is not only during our hours of sleep, but in many ways when we are awake; a tune, the smell of pipe tobacco or perfume, a television programme or perhaps a book can be used to get the message across, triggering something in our mind. A song might bring back important memories of a loved one. The words of that song may contain guidance to help us with an ongoing problem. A television play might mirror a situation in which we are involved, and by (unknowingly) being prompted by Spirit to watch the programme, we have been helped to deal with that situation.

Sometimes an idea will come to us seemingly out of thin air. The answer to our problem may occur to us as we are waking up, or something deep inside will stir a memory and all of a sudden the inspiration is there! Of course, when we develop the ability to communicate ourselves, the process is so much easier because then communication is a two-way track, but either way it is always of a positive nature.

Do we have to pay heed to what our spirit helpers are communicating to us?
No, we have free will, the freedom to choose. Free will is a gift that each of us can exercise. We each have the free will to make our own decisions, and we must make up our own minds. No one else can take on the responsibility for any decision we have made; it is our responsibility and ours alone. Thus, having free will, it follows that we have personal responsibility too. They walk hand in hand.

What does it mean to be constantly 'open to Spirit'?
When the majority of us first begin to communicate with our spirit helpers, we have to make a concerted effort to bring ourselves onto a higher wavelength so that our ordinary everyday thoughts do not intrude. One way of achieving this is to imagine travelling upwards towards the sun. When the communication is over, we bring ourselves down to earth by imagining walking down a very long spiral staircase step by step, until we reach the bottom. This is to prevent our minds going into 'overdrive'.

There are those who, for one reason or another, become involved in constant communication with Spirit. They are known as being 'open to Spirit' and need to understand that there is a need to discipline themselves to control this. There is a time and a place for everything in this life, and this applies to our time communicating with the Spirit World. It is important that people who are constantly 'open' should understand this and learn how to 'close themselves down' by using the method of the spiral staircase. If they do not do this, then their lives here can be in quite a confused state, spirit and earthly matters intermingling in an inappropriate way.

Discipline at all times is the key factor.

What does it mean "many are called; few are chosen"?
There are many, who for differing reasons, volunteer to come onto a planet. They have a calling – but those who are chosen

are asked to come in order to fulfil a special purpose in service to mankind.

The many who feel the calling to go to a planet do so for one or all of several reasons. Some wish to learn something in particular, some may wish to have a particular experience, and some may wish to be in service to mankind, to help the occupants of the planet or even the planet itself, taking it forward spiritually and technologically.

Whatever their reason, whatever their intention, unless their time on a planet is wasted in pursuit of something unspiritual, they should achieve spiritual progression. However, there is no certainty that they will realise their dream or purpose. They may be tempted to go in another direction and, having free will, there is nothing to prevent this. But walking every step of the way with them, whether they are walking the right or the wrong pathway, will be their guardian angel. When they start walking in the wrong direction, when temptation beckons and they give in, their guardian angel will do their utmost to persuade them to turn back and no matter what, their guardian angel will never stop trying to bring them back to the right road.

There is another, far smaller group who go to the planet with a purpose, who do not fall into the category of having been called. They are the special few, the few who have been chosen. They have been asked to go to the planet to complete a particular and very important task to take this planet forward spiritually and technologically. They are, of necessity spiritually evolved. Their mission is far too important for it to fail, so in order to ensure that they carry out the task for which they were chosen, they relinquish the right to free will during this lifetime; they give their permission for their free will to be overridden. There is a blueprint of their pathway and they do not deviate from it, come what may.

Are the place and the family into which we are born the 'luck of the draw'?
Spirit will always place us in a situation where the type of life

and experiences for our continued growth will best be served. Also, the talents we are to have during our time here will need a suitable environment where they can flower and be nurtured.

It may be that we have a talent for art but this does not necessarily mean that we will be born into an artistic family. Even so, the opportunity to develop that talent will arise; those from the Spirit World will guarantee this. If we are to be listeners and advisers, we will be placed in circumstances where we can learn and empathise with those who will need our help in the future.

How can the parents you have affect the type of person you become and the life you lead?
Firstly, you will inherit character traits from each of your parents so will have some of their strengths and weaknesses. The way your parents act, the example they set and the way they bring you up will all serve to affect the person you become. Also, the financial situation, education, careers and attitudes of your parents make quite an impression on you. Sometimes a tendency to dictate may have the opposite effect and cause you to rebel against their plans for you.

Is being born into a wealthy or talented family an advantage when following your chosen pathway?
This is not necessarily so. In one way the means to follow your chosen pathway could be made easier for you. For example, if you were to become a famous musician and had been born into a musical family, you would probably have the help and encouragement to develop your talent.

On the other hand, the strings they can pull because of the people they know, or influences they can wield, using their position in society, may be applied to prevent you from pursuing the pathway you wish to follow. They may wish you to join the family business or follow in your mother or father's footsteps, which may be far from the direction that you wish to go. Or it may be made too easy for you; there is far more to learn by achieving things on your own.

If your pathway is to help those less fortunate than yourself, not having experienced their suffering or hardship will make it much harder for you to appreciate how difficult life is for them. It may also engender a feeling of superiority where others are concerned, and as a result stifle your understanding and communication with them.

For what reason might we be born into a situation where poverty, even famine, war or other terrible conditions exist?
This may be to enable you to experience extreme suffering and to learn from it or even to do something towards alleviating the problems that exist there.

"Cometh the hour, cometh the man (or woman)." Prophets and masters throughout the history of this planet, Ghandi, Churchill, Moses, Joan of Arc, Mother Teresa, Buddha, Jesus, Mohammed and many others came at a time when their special gifts, spirituality and leadership were desperately needed in this world. They were born at the time and place where they could be most effective. But many people have been involved, unknown and unsung, in helping others in extreme conditions and they too will be acclaimed upon their return to the Spirit World.

Why are people born with disabilities?
This may be because of a defective gene, or perhaps something going wrong either when the cells of the fertilised egg are dividing, or during the birth. Alternatively it may be because a spirit has asked specifically to spend a life as a disabled person. This could be because they wish to have that experience to give them the opportunity to overcome it and grow strong from it. It could also be to help others to grow, by giving them the opportunity to develop love and compassion in their dealings with the person's disability.

If we come to this planet to follow a pathway, why is it that many people do not appear to be doing so?
How do you know they are not? We cannot all be great masters or reformers. For most of us just living an ordinary life, minding our own business and trying not to do harm to others is sufficient. Spiritual growth does not necessarily happen in quantum leaps, but is hopefully a slow and steady progression. After all, we have forever to work at it.

There are of course, times when a significant advance appears to be made. Sometimes where a child has problems and where there does not seem to be any help for them, this inspires parents or friends to initiate a charity or self-help group. Sometimes a complete lifestyle change happens when people give up lucrative jobs to start working and helping those less fortunate than themselves.

These changes can happen quite late in life for some people because they may have needed experiences which will be used to help them along their new pathway.

We must not forget that Spirit are behind many of these happenings. Our helpers can impress us at the right point in our lives to make the change our spirit has always intended to make – much to our surprise at times. How often do we hear, "When I was younger I would never have dreamed of doing what I am now"?

Do we have an allotted life span?
Yes. This is allocated by Spirit in accordance with what we hope to achieve during this physical life.

Can we go beyond it?
No. Our life span was decided when our pathway was planned and it cannot be extended. No form of healing, operation, drug, prayer or the preservation of the body will affect this prearranged event; it is not in our hands but in the hands of those in the Spirit World.

Can we go before our allotted time?
Yes. There are no guarantees; the responsibility is ours. Self-neglect and not taking care in everyday life can lead to both illness and premature death. An accident may also terminate life earlier than was planned. In addition to this, you may choose to take your own life, or someone could end it for you by an act of violence.

However, there is a small number of people who, no matter what happens will not go before their time. They are those who have been chosen by Spirit to come here for an important, specific purpose to help mankind and the planet to go forward spiritually, scientifically and technologically. These lovely spirits have relinquished their free will during this incarnation to enable Spirit to ensure they complete their task. Spirit will afford them special protection on this occasion only and they will not leave the planet until their allotted time arrives and their mission is accomplished.

What makes us feel more comfortable with ourselves when the spirit passes out of the physical body?
As the spirit is leaving the physical body it takes on the appearance of the body that we have just occupied, because we are unfamiliar with the sight of pure spirit, and might feel ill at ease with this new image of ourselves.

Is our guardian angel there to meet us?
Our guardian angel is almost certainly unknown to us up to this point because our mind is still locked, so would not be recognised, and therefore remains in the background while our loved ones come forward to greet us. If we have no loved ones at all to greet us, then loving spirits will meet us to take us back to the Spirit World.

Once our mind is unlocked then we will be able to recognise our guardian angel as a member of our spirit family and they will come forward to greet us and be reunited.

What is your conscience?
Conscience is your moral sense linked with your guardian angel, who works hard to get you to understand when you are doing something wrong.

Some people do not appear to have a conscience. Can that be so?
Everyone has a conscience, but many are so insensitive to others that it is easy for them to brush it aside. At all times their guardian angel tries to get them to see right from wrong; that is their duty, but everyone has free will, and if they do not wish to listen, they cannot be impelled to do so.

Is it true that we are all brothers and sisters under the skin?
Yes, it is true, although many people still have great difficulty in accepting this. We are all spirits temporarily housed in a physical body. We have come from the Spirit World, a world of love and harmony. While we are there we are still individuals with our own point of view, likes and dislikes.

So how do we live together without dissension? We don't, but by using the great love and wisdom we have, and drawing upon greater knowledge and guidance available from the elders of the Spirit World, we are able to disagree agreeably.

While we are here on the planet we have to deal with problems and pressures not experienced in the Spirit World. We have the lack of understanding between those of different races, cultures and religions. There is competition for food and materials, and at times the need for more space to house our expanding population. In addition, the majority of us are ignorant of the fact that we are spiritual beings and are unaware of the reasons why we are here in the first place.

It can be seen therefore what a difficult task it is for us to live together in love and harmony as brothers and sisters. Our only hope is that by working together we will at some time in the future achieve something like the ideal world that is the world of spirit.

Is it wrong to hate another?

Not only is it wrong, it is also harmful. When you harbour feelings of hatred and bitterness, you stunt your soul growth and generally affect your physical wellbeing. Hate-filled thoughts sent to another often rebound and cause the sender further bitterness. If someone does something that you find impossible to forgive, then try to find it within yourself to feel sorry for them. The day will come when they will have to obtain your forgiveness, and they will suffer far more than you have suffered. Feeling sorry – compassion – is a form of love, and once you can send out love, you will find that you will be the benefactor and will be able to move on.

How can we help others to grow?

Firstly we can help those who are in a physical body by giving them the chance to show kindness and compassion to us when we are in need, and everyone in the physical world is in need at one time or another, whether it be materially, emotionally or physically. When we ask another for help, they have the choice of whether to respond to our request or not. If they do, they learn and grow; we have given them that opportunity.

Secondly, we can help those in the Spirit World to grow too. We each have spirit helpers working with us from the Astral Plane and the most prominent of these is our guardian angel, who is there by our side every step of the way.

Unknown to us, our guardian angels give us advice on a regular basis and, when necessary, counselling. When we ignore them and go our own way, they need and develop patience and forbearance. Dealing with our weaknesses and our shortcomings, they also develop great tolerance and understanding, and their love grows while filling such a demanding role.

They learn with us by witnessing our mistakes. They teach us to use the love within us to help others, and they persevere to break through the barriers that our closed minds erect.

When their service to us is over, they will recognise that they have grown spiritually too.

Are some people 'born bad'?
When we are placed in the womb we are pure spirit, and no spirit is bad. Different influences throughout our lives can affect the way we behave, but that is up to us. There is good and bad in all of us, but it is up to us to bring the good to the fore at all times. We – and nobody else – are responsible for our actions for we have free will and can decide which way we wish to go.

Many historical figures have used their power in the wrong way. They allowed bad traits such as greed, selfishness, corruption etc. to overcome the good. But once they returned to the Spirit World, a world of love, they would have recognised what good they *could* have done, and would have felt such anguish and deep remorse that it would be almost too much for them to bear. They would try to make amends through love.

Can it be in someone's plan to commit murder?
No, nothing of an unspiritual nature is ever part of anyone's plan. And Spirit will work hard to try to prevent any act of violence. But everyone has free will and that includes the free will to do evil as well as to act in a caring and spiritual way.

Is suicide planned?
No death – other than the death at the end of a life span – is planned. No one comes here to murder or be murdered, and no one comes here to commit suicide. We all have our pathway to tread, but depending upon how we cope with the various problems it brings, whether we deviate from that pathway, our general character and state of mind will dictate whether we bring ourselves to the point of suicide

Questions and Answers on the Astral Plane

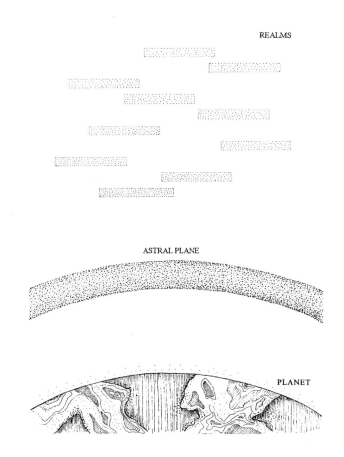

Please note that this is purely a symbolic representation and not an illustration

The void between a planet and the spirit realms is immense, and direct communication between them is not possible. In order to overcome this problem, the Spirit World has placed with every planet that supports life what is known as an "Astral Plane." This is used as a stepping-stone back to the Spirit World. This plane also provides a base, a workstation, for those from the Spirit World who wish to help us, who are in a physical body.

Where is the Spirit World?

While we are in a physical body our minds are unable to even grasp the physics of the Spirit World. Once we leave our physical body, we will be taken there by our loved ones who are waiting for us, and who are in service to mankind. Having left the physical body at death, our lack of understanding of the Spirit World is unchanged and will remain so until we return there.

Isn't the Spirit World around us?

No. Spirits are constantly around us but the actual whereabouts of the Spirit World is unknown to us.

Is the Spirit World what we call Heaven?

Heaven, Paradise, the Garden of Eden, Nirvana, Valhalla etc. – there are many names we call the place to which we return after physical death. But whatever we choose to call it, it is the spiritual home of *everyone* regardless of race, beliefs and the way they have led their life. There is no discrimination.

What is it like?

Until we return home we cannot visualise it, but we are told it is a place of love, light and beauty. The only part of the Spirit World of which we have some knowledge is the Astral Plane. We know that this is a carbon copy of the planet but without the dross and darkness.

Why does the Astral Plane resemble the planet?

This is because it contributes to the easement of our transition from the planet to the Spirit World. We feel comfortable with the familiar surroundings and the next stage is approached without fear or confusion. There is no possibility of our feeling lost or alone within these conditions and we are accompanied by our loved ones every step of the way.

What is the Astral Plane?

It is the first place to which each of us goes when we return to the Spirit World.

Each planet has its own Astral Plane that resembles the physical planet to which it belongs.

What happens when we arrive on the Astral Plane?

We are taken to a kind of reception centre where the spirit goes through a form of rest, healing and readjustment to enable us to recover from the draining experience of having had a physical life, and to lose the taint of earthly matter. During this process, the very important part of resettlement is the unlocking of the mind and the restoration of its full power. It is then that we reflect on the life we have just led, coming to terms with how we dealt with it.

Once my mind is unlocked, does my character change?

Once your mind is unlocked you are again the real you. This means that you are free of the physical influences i.e. astrological, environmental and genetic characteristics that affected your personality whilst you were in a physical body. However, although you will now be able to see things from a different and more spiritual perspective, you will still feel the hurts that have been inflicted upon you during your physical life. It will take a while for you to recover and to forgive. In addition to this, there will have been instances when you've hurt another and it will also take time for you to earn their forgiveness and to forgive yourself.

Despite the fact that their mind has been unlocked, a person of strong character convinced of the rightness of their actions will still adhere to that belief and may well need gentle persuasion to look within more deeply to recognise and accept the deficiencies of the life they led.

How long does the process of healing and readjustment take?

For as long as it takes. It all depends upon how depleted the spirit is when it passes out of the physical body. In the cases of someone who lived to a ripe old age, someone whose body was subjected to lifelong abuse or a series of illnesses, or someone whose passing was traumatic, then the healing, readjustment and subsequent return to former strength would take considerably longer than perhaps someone who died younger without a long or draining illness. The younger the physical body was on passing, the less time there is needed for the healing of the spirit. Note that it is the *spirit body* that is healed, as there is no longer a physical body needing attention. The spirit needs this healing because a period of physical pain and suffering while in a physical body also takes its toll on the spirit.

Are there different levels on the Astral Plane?

Yes. There is a need to separate those of different levels of spirituality. Everyone goes to the level upon which they are acceptable. A person who in physical life was cruel, brutal or ruthless cannot be with those who led a decent life. The more spiritual we are, the higher the level to which we go while on the Astral Plane. For those who are working in spiritual service to those on the Earth there will be an appropriate level on the Astral Plane from which to work.

Please do not confuse the levels on the Astral Plane with the spirit realms. They are very different places.

Does everyone go to the |Astral Plane after death?
Yes – eventually. We still have free will and if we do not wish to leave the Earth Plane after our physical death, then we can remain on the earth for as long as we wish. We will be earthbound and will have lost the physical powers that we had while in a physical body. The only power we will have is the same limited power of our mind to impress our thoughts onto others of the same light – those whose spirituality is of the same level as our own - or those of a lower light, bearing in mind that everyone has free will and can reject these thoughts.

However long we choose to stay earthbound the day will come when we will make the decision to take that journey to the Astral Plane. Everyone goes there sooner or later, no matter how long they choose to remain here.

Is it true that you can be reborn shortly after your death and begin a new life here?
No one can return to this or any other planet and be reborn for hundreds of years after they have passed from a physical body. This is the law of the Spirit World. Otherwise our loved ones would not be able to be there to greet us when we pass from the physical body, and we would not have the opportunity to be reunited with our spirit family.

When we leave the Earth Plane to go to the Astral Plane, this is often referred to as being reborn. Perhaps this is why people believe that we can be placed in a womb to be reincarnated shortly after physical death.

Note that there are those who are not allowed to return to a planet even after hundreds of years.

Upon my return to the spirit realm, will I sever all connections with, and interest in this planet?
Upon your arrival on the Astral Plane you may be given the opportunity to stay there for a period to work with those on this planet. Eventually all the close members of your physical family will have joined you there, and you will

then think of returning to your spirit realm.

But you will still take a close interest in this planet because members of your *spirit* family may still be working here or from the Astral Plane, as you have done.

Can we choose to remain on the planet after we have left the physical body?

The pull of the physical family is so strong that sometimes we may wish to remain with them for a while, especially if our loved ones are so consumed by grief that they are finding it hard to carry on.

A young family left behind, or a partner who is finding it hard to cope with their loss, can inadvertently keep their loved one close when they should be back in the Spirit World regaining their strength. When the ones who have passed understand that they will be of more help to those they have left behind once they have gone to the Spirit World to have their power restored, they can usually be persuaded to go there.

Can anything else delay our journey to the Astral Plane?

Yes, several things:

Fear can keep someone 'earthbound' for a long time. Some religions that preach hell and damnation for every transgression are responsible for many being too frightened to leave the Earth Plane because they fear what will happen to them.

The love of material things and not being able to bear the thought of leaving them, or of someone else owning them, can keep some tied to the earth for a little while.

Unfinished business e.g. a son or daughter's wedding, the birth of a long awaited child, someone close attaining a degree, diploma, prize etc., or someone whose life was ended by another wishing to see justice take its course. All can serve to delay a departure for the Spirit World.

Distrust of those who come to meet them. If they have been unfortunate in their life to suffer at the hands of others, and have had no reason to trust another person, then when they have passed out of their body, again they are unlikely to believe they can trust those who have come to meet them.

Fear of meeting someone who, in their earthly life, had been cruel or unkind to them. The depth of fear may override any reassurances that have been given that they do *not* have to meet such a person. If their strength of mind is such that they cannot bring themselves to accept this, then they could remain earthbound for quite a long time.

Should we remain earthbound, what would our guardian angel do?
Once our guardian angel has cut the silver cord, their job is done. They will then return to the Spirit World.

In all cases, those from the Spirit World will never cease in their endeavours to bring everyone over to the Astral Plane. *Everyone*, however long it may take, will return to the Spirit World.

When our full power has been restored to us, in what ways may we be of service while working from the Astral Plane?
Working alongside those in service to mankind e.g. scientists, surgeons, musicians, artists etc.

Helping this planet to go forward spiritually and technologically.

Counselling those who have been traumatised by the method of their passing e.g. sudden death.

As a spiritual healer and philosopher.

As a guardian angel.

Helping with spiritual guidance.

Working in the team that takes young children to the Astral Plane.

Taking the spirit of a very young baby or foetus over to the Astral Plane

Looking after the animals on the planet.

Looking after the planet...............And many, many more.

If we are working from the Astral Plane, do we get the chance to rest?
Yes. You will not need rest in the way that you need it when in a physical body as you will not be *physically* tired. However, there will be occasions when you need to take a step back from a situation. You can be emotionally overworked and drained.

How long do we remain on the Astral Plane?
It varies but not usually longer than 100 years unless you are the guardian angel of someone who lives to be 110! When your job is complete you will be more than ready to leave the Astral Plane and return to your true spiritual home.

If someone took their own life, would they be allowed to work from the Astral Plane?
Spirit does not look upon suicide as a sin, as in some cultures. It is merely an escape from life when it became too much for that person to bear. As they leave behind the burden of their physical body with its muddled thinking, and have their mind unlocked, the great disappointment in themselves that they will feel will be punishment enough for them. Unless during their life on the planet they were really wicked, or were responsible for somebody's death, they would be permitted to work in service from the Astral Plane, some perhaps to help to prevent other potential suicides.

What happens to spirits who have led a life of wickedness? Are they punished?
Once they have rested and had their mind unlocked and their power restored, they are returned to their spirit realm, as they are not allowed to remain on the Astral Plane. They will not be judged by anyone else or receive the form of punishment that would be recognised on Earth. But they do not escape judgement, for they will judge themselves, and because the Spirit World is a world of love they will judge themselves more harshly than anyone else could. They will realise the enormity

of what they have done. They will be horrified, deeply ashamed, and full of remorse. They will want to show this remorse through love, and will work hard to obtain forgiveness from all those they have hurt. Once that has been attained, and it could take a very long time, they will put themselves into a state of purgatory until they can at last forgive themselves. This also could take a very long time.

The process from beginning to end is intricate and involved and cannot be fully appreciated from this account.

Can a spirit come down to the Astral Plane straight from a spirit realm?

No. It is necessary for a spirit already in the Spirit World to touch the Earth Plane before being able to work from the Astral Plane, even if it is only briefly i.e. as a foetus or very young baby. When spirits are in the Spirit World living in their realm, they are very sensitive and refined. Consequently they are too refined and sensitive to come directly from their realm to work from the Astral Plane with those on the Earth Plane.

There is a need to lose this sensitivity, and this is achieved during the process of preparation (whatever that may be) before the spirit is planted in the womb. Once having touched the Earth Plane - briefly or otherwise - they lose a lot of their sensitivity and refinement. Having been placed in the womb they then become affected by the dross of the physical body, therefore finding it easier, on reaching the Astral Plane after physical death, to relate to and work with those living on the Earth Plane.

What is different when a baby or foetus passes out of their physical form?

A foetus or a very young baby is as they were when put into the womb, with a mind that is empty. Thus they have no recognition or understanding of anything physical. Their passing from their physical body is therefore an immediate reversion to the spirit form. There is no question of their having to make a decision whether or not to remain on the Earth Plane. They are taken by someone from the Spirit World whose service it is to look after babies. They are cocooned in love, and carried 'home'. They will then go through the same process of healing and readjustment in the Spirit World as everyone else does.

When a child passes, it is quite possible that they do not recall any family member who has passed to the Spirit World before them. Who will meet them?
Although the child may not know the faces of family who have already passed, they will still be there to meet them. Besides, members of their physical family, the welcoming party will also include those from the Astral Plane who have chosen to work with love and patience to gain the child's trust in order to take it back home. Children will be taken by whoever they feel drawn to and with whom they feel most comfortable. This may be someone from their physical family or someone who works specifically to take babies and children over. In doing this they are ensuring that the law of the Spirit World is adhered to regarding the safety of children.

Do children who have passed to the Spirit World grow up in that world as child spirits?
No. Growing up is physical. Once returned to the Spirit World children revert to being themselves - pure spirit. However, if a physical life is shortened accidentally and the child was not meant to die, then they may choose to come back to 'shadow' a child of the same age in order to observe and learn from the experiences of the child as it grows. In all probability, the child will be aware of their presence during their childhood and may refer to their 'friend'.

Children who have passed never detach themselves from those of their physical family whom they have loved and who still love and miss them but the roles are now reversed and the child is the one who comforts and seeks to help and protect the members of their physical family.

Why have people been told that their children are growing up in the Spirit World?

This impression is given because they have the power to show themselves at an age beyond that of their passing. In doing so it gives a little comfort to their grieving parents.

Why is it that children seem to be able to 'see' spirits when adults can't?

This is because children have not yet learned to distrust what they see, are not cynical and are not able to search for a reason to dismiss what they can see before their eyes. As they grow older and their lives become more complicated they lose their innocence, and tend to lose the ability to 'see' Spirit.

Why are children sometimes seen playing with spirit children?

Those on the Astral Plane can adopt the image of the form they have previously had as their own, and those who passed as children can still show themselves as the child. When you see spirit children, it is the spirit taking on the image that was their own, and they are playing with the earth child in order to bring happiness to that child.

At times there is a need for grieving parents to be reassured that they have not lost their child. To see their child, to know they still exist and are playing with or are friends of other children that are here in the physical body, brings some peace of mind to the parent.

What could be the reason for not being aware of a loved one's return to the Earth Plane after they have passed on?

There are several reasons why loved ones do not appear to have contacted their families.

They may be ashamed of the way they behaved when in the physical body and are unable to face them.

They may have come close, but because their family knows nothing of the Spirit World or their grief has blotted out everything else, they may have been unaware of their presence.

Having them constantly in their thoughts even when they do draw close, they would not recognise the difference.

Soon after they passed they may have volunteered to serve as guardian angels. Prior to taking up their duty they would be involved in preparation for the role they are about to play.

These are a few of the reasons but there are others.

If when we are on the Astral Plane we need a rest from the work with those on the planet, is there other work that we may do?
There is plenty of work to be done. There are those who help spirits returning from the planet, those giving healing to exhausted spirits, and then counselling them as they come to terms with their last life.

Also, those who are working on the planet need back up too from time to time. If you wish to work there will always be something of interest to do.

Questions and Answers on Group Spirits

What are we and where do we come from?

We are spirit, have always been spirit and always will be spirit. We are indestructible; we are infinite. But the process of creation is beyond our comprehension while we are in a physical body, for at this time we have only limited powers of understanding.

We do know that we are all created as individuals and are an integral part of the God power. Even as individuals we have a part of the God power within us - our spirituality - and thus wherever we are, so too is the God power. The light, that part of the God power that is within everyone, will never go out regardless of whatever wrong we may do. It may go so dim as to become just a spark but we will always have the opportunity to right the wrong we have committed and to increase that light, the spirituality within, by living life in a more spiritual way. The strength of our light shows the measure of our spirituality.

Were all spirits created at the same time?

No. They were created in spirit family groups at various times and will remain as spirit family groups throughout eternity.

Where does the spirit group go when created?

It goes to the first spirit realm and progresses from there. Initially the members of the spirit group are unevolved and will be helped by spirits from higher realms to gain sufficient mental and emotional development in order to prepare for the experience of living in a physical body on a planet. They go to a physical planet which is suitable for their level of understanding, and which will provide the experience they require to start on their spiritual journey, and thus to eventually progress to higher realms.

Do we belong to the same family group when we return to the Spirit World?

The family to which we belong when in the physical body, and the one to which we belong when in the Spirit World can be very different. The family members of our many physical lives can change and vary, but we each belong to our own *spirit* family, which never changes, from our creation throughout eternity. It is when we are once again back with our spirit family that we understand the true meaning of family, loving and working to help each other, for we all have a common aim and that is to progress together to still higher realms and the spiritual rewards that await us there.

Who or what is a soul mate?
Within each spirit family, every member will have what we refer to as a soul mate. They are created as partners and will remain so throughout eternity. They are separated when they have work to do, each progressing along their own spiritual pathways. The love between these two spirits is greater than any other love, and gets stronger throughout eternity. They are completely compatible – two halves of a whole, but at all times they remain the individual. Although there is no gender, as we understand the male and female body here, there is a difference linked with the spiritual body, which can only be understood by us when we return to the Spirit World.

Are we usually married to our soul mate?
No, not usually but it can happen. Should this eventuality occur it is highly unlikely that you would be aware of it; your physical partnership will be much as that of anyone else. You may even become incompatible whilst in the marriage, but upon your being together once more in the Spirit World your love for each other will overcome this temporary hiccup in your journey together.

Why do some people in their physical life feel they have met their soul mate?
This is because they are so compatible, are on the same wavelength and the same level of understanding. They feel a close affinity to each other. But the love that they have

for each other, no matter how great, is only an earthly love however spiritual that may be. The love between soul mates is a spiritual love of such power and beauty that it is something that we in our physical bodies cannot even imagine.

Is it possible for any of the spirits belonging to the group to reach a higher level of understanding than the rest of the group?

Yes, it most certainly is. Those who have worked hard in their spiritual service can reach a greater spiritual understanding than perhaps other members of the group have had the opportunity to do. But there is no unfairness in the Spirit World; there will always be the opportunity for every member of the group or family, to reach the same level.

Those who have progressed further than the rest of the group will not move up to another realm in advance of the other members. The family remains together throughout eternity and would not wish it otherwise. Everyone moves as one family. Those who have reached a higher level of spiritual understanding are in a position to advise and encourage the others to reach the level required, but always remember that each one must achieve this on their own.

Are there leaders in each spirit family?

As in any group on earth, there are always those who learn more quickly and reach targets first and it is so within each spirit family. Those who have reached that higher level of spiritual understanding, act as elders and give their advice.

Is every spirit family on the same level of spiritual understanding?

No. Spirit families are all on varying levels of spiritual development and understanding, with each individual within the family unit working towards spiritual growth.

Once each member of the group has reached the appropriate level of spiritual understanding, then the family is ready to move, but this does not happen until all members have returned to their present realm and they are all there together. The move is a reason for celebration, and is completed as a happy family occasion. But be aware that the work involved to merit this move will not be easy.

The length of time we spend on each realm varies, but we do not need to concern ourselves with this as we have eternity in which to evolve.

If we are perfectly happy living on our realm in the Spirit World, why do we subject ourselves to the trauma of a physical life?
As we understand it from our limited knowledge of the Spirit World, it is a beautiful place where the problems associated with a physical life do not exist. We are told that the reason why we come to a planet is to further our spiritual growth. Because so many of us come here, there must be a very compelling reason why. It is certainly not pressure imposed upon us by our fellow spirits. It is a world of love, and they would not try to force us to come here against our will.

We know already that when all those in a spirit group reach a certain level they are able to move up to a higher spiritual realm. It is apparent that the advantages gained by coming here outweigh the disadvantages, and that adding to our spiritual growth brings rewards we are not aware of whilst we are here. That knowledge acts as the spur for us to keep striving towards that growth.

But please bear in mind that not everyone returns to the spirit realm more spiritual than when they left.

Will your physical family belong to the same spirit group as you?
Not necessarily. It is all according to the experience you need for this physical life. There are times when the Spirit World has special work to be done on a planet, and members of a *spirit* family will work together as members of the same *physical*

family. Sometimes even family friends will be members of that spirit family, working closely on the same spiritual project.

Is it correct that spirits are created bad, and have to work towards getting better?
No, a newly created spirit is of course unevolved but, coming from the Spirit World, will have only experienced a loving environment and will be as a blank page in a book, innocent and ready to learn. All spirits are created in love and all have an equal chance to grow spiritually.

Is it true that if you were bad in the last life, you will suffer in the next?
No, this is quite untrue. You will certainly have to make up for any wrongs that you do in one life but if you do not put them right in that life, you will have to work at putting them right once you have returned to the Spirit World. No one can forgive your sins except those whom you have wronged, which may take a very long time. When eventually you have been forgiven for those wrongs you have done, you have to work to forgive yourself, which is very difficult indeed. You are living in a world of love, and the shame that you feel at what you have done is tremendous.

Having been forgiven by the victims of your wrong doing and also by yourself, then in time – and it could be a very, very long time – you may be allowed to return to a planet to live another physical life and have the opportunity to grow spiritually. What has occurred in the past remains in the past. You have made retribution; there is nothing more to pay.

What is the difference between a very evolved spirit i.e. spiritually advanced, and one that is less evolved?
The evolved spirit has achieved greater mind and soul growth, which comes from experiences gained through different incarnations. Therefore they can be chosen to carry out special tasks that Spirit consider necessary for the spiritual growth

of this planet. At times this can be extremely hard, but their evolvement and the support from the Spirit World will ensure that their work is completed.

Why do some people seem to have an easy life while others appear to have nothing but problems, pain and suffering?
Those who appear to have a difficult life may do so for two different reasons. They may have wished for a harder life in order to learn, and by so doing increase their spiritual understanding. Alternatively, they may have brought their problems on themselves by their own actions.

Those who seem to have an easy ride do not necessarily have a life that is as trouble free as it would seem; nobody really knows what is going on in another's life. However, an easier life may be all one particular person is ready for at that time, while others are able and ready to learn from a life full of hardship.

Is suffering essential for the divine plan?
There are certain rare cases where a spirit has requested that the physical body they occupy when on the planet is crippled, or that it will suffer from a disease or illness that mankind has yet to cure. This is because that spirit wishes to serve mankind in such a brave and unselfish way that by their suffering the doctors and scientists are able to learn, and in so doing help others who in the future will suffer in the same way. They are also able to help others to expand their soul growth by giving them the opportunity to show compassion, and help by looking after them.

However, for the rest of us, a lot of our suffering has been brought upon us by ourselves. If we learn and grow from that suffering, then that has been of benefit to us.

Where the divine plan is involved, there may be plans for us to enter into a relationship or situation which will present problems to be solved, and challenges to be met. This may involve suffering. It all depends upon the situation and how we deal with it. Suffering is not essential to the divine plan.

Would you always expect an evolved spirit to appear spiritual in their earthly life?
No. Spirit growth does not necessarily show itself whilst in a physical body. Such things as the traits they have inherited from their physical parents, astrological influences and the environment in which they live, affect the character of the person and these can overshadow their spiritual evolvement.

Is the sex you are in this life part of the plan, and decided beforehand?
If you are meant to be a certain sex for a particular reason, nothing or no one can change it, but there are times when it could be the "luck of the draw."

Are you always the same sex when in a physical body?
No, your sex is the one that is appropriate for the experience you need to have to aid your spiritual progression.

Is there a part of us that remains in the Spirit World when we are living on a planet?
No. Your spirit could not exist without your mind and soul. They are an integral part of the spirit in the same way that the heart and the brain are an integral part of the physical body. Accepting that the spirit cannot be extinguished, the spirit, mind and soul cannot be separated.

What may have led to this idea is the 'locking' of the mind before we came to this planet. But although we do not have access to a certain part of the mind and knowledge and wisdom stored there, it is still with us, in our spirit wherever we may be.

The only part of us that may *seem* to be left behind in the Spirit World is our soul mate, for although we are individuals in our own right, when we are with our soul mate it is then that we really feel whole.

During a physical life, we will have opportunities to learn, improve and expand many different aspects of our spiritual selves, using both the mind and the soul.

Do we have spirit names in the Spirit World?
We do not have names as we would understand the term. However, we do have a form of identity that is known to others but what format that may take, we will only know when we are back in the Spirit World.

Questions and Answers on the Mind

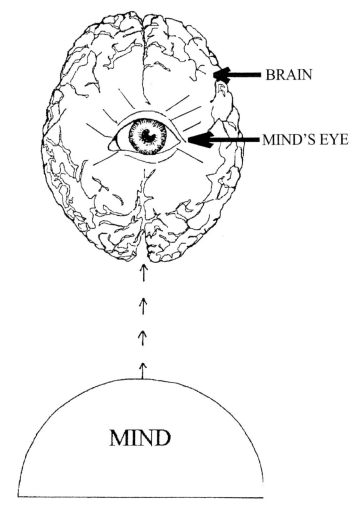

BRAIN

MIND'S EYE

MIND

Again, this is purely a symbolic representation

Our mind is the most powerful tool we have on this planet. We may be in awe of the majesty and power of our own creations, the nuclear bomb, the space rockets, the supertankers, the skyscrapers, but these are but creations of our mind. These in their turn are dwarfed by the power of nature, the creation of the God power.

We can use the mind to create or destroy. Our way of thinking determines our disposition and affects our physical condition.

Negative thinking opens the way to illness (dis-ease) for we must never forget that thought is a force that can damage body and spirit, and even destroy our physical body.

We must avoid, if we can, those who transmit negative thoughts, those who are full of hatred, envy, egotism and jealousy. We must use our mind to create positive thoughts to uplift ourselves, and those around us too. We have been given a mind to use; we must use it wisely with all the wisdom, common sense and love at our command.

***

Where is the mind?
It is contained within the spirit and is part of the spirit and as such is indestructible; but in relation to the physical body, it is located in the area of the chest.

What is the relationship between the mind and the brain?
Whereas all thoughts are created in the mind, the brain is a computer that receives and acts on these thoughts to motivate the physical body.

What is the difference between the brain and the mind?
The mind is part of the spirit, whereas the brain is part of the physical body. The mind within the spirit goes on into eternity, but the brain dies when the physical body dies.

What is responsible for our thoughts and our actions, the mind or the brain?

Both. The mind is part of the spirit and produces every thought, every idea and every inspiration that we have. They are then sent to that part of the physical body that will receive, interpret and transmit the message – the brain.

The brain is a powerful organ. It is very complicated, and mankind has still much to learn about its different functions. But enough is known for it to be understood that messages sent from the mind are not always transmitted from the brain in the form that they were intended.

There is a part of the brain which affects the behaviour pattern and certain elements can bring about a character change, turn Jekyll into Hyde. If the volume of certain chemicals that are present in the brain is changed – if there is too much or too little – then this can have quite a dramatic effect on the character. Similarly a brain tumour, a stroke, or an accident affecting that part of the brain can also be responsible for a character change. In addition to this, taking drugs or drinking alcohol can have the same effect.

When those in the Spirit World wish to communicate with us, they draw close to the mind and send the communication mind to mind. If we are not receptive, do not wish to receive such communication, then we can block it out of the mind and ignore it. How many times, on reflection, have we wished we had listened to that inner voice?

Spirit is around us all the time, helping, advising and influencing us. But we are not necessarily aware of this; most times their efforts are in vain, or that inner voice is ignored. It is important that we learn how to communicate with our spirit helpers, to open ourselves up in a natural way, and eventually to be able to have a two-way conversation with them when the motive is right, when the conversation is with a view to helping to sort out a problem, or to help someone else.

Are thoughts living things, and can they be destroyed?
Yes, thoughts are living things but they cannot be destroyed. Once a thought comes into the mind, it remains there and becomes part of the mind. Because the mind cannot be destroyed, neither can the thought. Every thought returns with us to the Spirit World.

Is it possible for another person to read our thoughts?
Most certainly not. Our thoughts are private. Only our guardian angel and those who work with us from the Spirit World know what is going on in our mind, because it is their job to know, in order to guide our thoughts in the right direction. Our loved ones, who have passed to the Spirit World and still love and care about us, are also privy to our thoughts so that they can help us in whatever way they can.

However, unknowingly we can spell out our thoughts to others here on the planet just by the way we sit, stand, move, and also the look in our eyes. Anyone who can read our body language has a good idea of what we are thinking. They haven't read our mind, just our body.

There are also occasions when Spirit have impressed upon us how a person is feeling in order that we may understand and be of help to them.

The Spirit World is a world of thought, so does that mean that our thoughts can be read when we are there?
Again the answer is no. This would be an invasion of privacy and of our free will to keep something to ourselves. Our thoughts are our own until we wish to share them with others. We will then project them, but only to those whom we wish to receive them.

What is the relationship between the soul and the mind?
They interact. There is no thought without a feeling, and no feeling without a thought.

What is the mind's eye?
The mind's eye is an extension of the mind, rather like a periscope, which enables the mind to work with the physical brain.

Where is it?
When in operation, it is located in the middle of the forehead and has been referred to as the third eye

What is its function?
It relays messages between the mind and the brain. It is a two-way process. All thoughts sent to and from the brain go via the mind's eye. It is usually in action during our waking hours only but sometimes it is opened in the moments before waking, when there is a need for a dream to be transmitted to the brain to be recalled upon regaining full consciousness. The mind's eye extends to a position in front of the brain and from there transmits the messages to and fro.

As there is only a need to send messages to a brain when we are in a physical body, there is no use for the mind's eye when we are pure spirit in the Spirit World. Thus it remains within the mind, superfluous until such time as we embark on another physical life.

Is it possible to 'stretch' the mind's eye?
Yes it is. We do this whenever we think hard about something, whenever we try to work something out, when we are creating, expanding our thoughts and when we open our minds to link with our spirit helpers.

What is the difference between the mind's eye and the physical eye?
The mind's eye is of the spirit and cannot be seen. The physical eye is part of the physical body.

What kind of person would have considerable mind expansion?
Somebody who thinks a lot, who seeks information and acquires wisdom.

Is it better to have great mind expansion or a large soul growth?
Neither. You should aim at all times to balance mind and soul growth.

How can soul growth affect our ability to expand the mind?
If we allow our feelings to rule our thinking – letting the heart rule the head – then our thoughts are not clear and mind growth is stifled. Feelings are governed by our soul, and if we allow those feelings to become too strong without corresponding mind expansion, our feelings will control our thinking too.

Soul growth and mind expansion should progress side by side balancing our thoughts and our actions.

Is the mind divided up into different compartments like the brain?
It is necessary to envisage a symbolic picture of the mind divided into four parts.

One part, which eventually becomes the largest part of all, contains the wisdom gained from knowledge of the Spirit World and our past experiences from previous lives. This is the part that is locked before we begin a physical life.

The other compartments all relate to our present life:

The past subconscious contains all our thoughts to date during our present incarnation, no matter how trivial.

The present conscious is very small and contains the thoughts we are having at the moment, thoughts which quickly pass into the past subconscious part of the mind as another thought comes to take their place.

The final part of the mind is the future subconscious.

Stored here are the thoughts placed into our mind without our knowledge, which are kept until such time that we need them in order to deal with a sensitive situation yet to come. We do not always make use of these thoughts because we may use our free will to do things our own way.

Information is fed into our future subconscious mind during sleep. Sometimes we receive it when we converse with our spirit helpers but forget it on waking. On other occasions it is given to us as a dream which we do not recall. Many people have experienced what is known as déjà vu. This is an instant when you know already what is about to be said or done. Again Spirit have placed this information in the future subconscious part of the mind, and the event or words will trigger its release. This, unlike our dreams and other forms of counselling, serves no purpose except to illustrate how Spirit can work with our mind.

Do we bring all our wisdom with us to each life?
The wisdom we have accumulated during different incarnations is stored in the mind, and is there when we enter another life. However, we cannot use this information while in this life because it is locked away and we do not have access to it until during the readjustment process on the Astral Plane, when this part of the mind is unlocked. The reason why this information is locked away from us is because we could not cope with, or even comprehend, all the information stored there with the limited powers of understanding that we have while in a physical body and it would confuse our life here.

Is the soul locked in a similar way?
No. Whatever feelings of love and compassion we have accumulated during past incarnations is brought with us to each life. But this does not necessarily result in the expression of our compassion. Genetic, astrological and environmental influences can affect us to such an extent that they override our basic goodness and kindness.

The social attitudes of the country in which we live can also inhibit an expression of compassion. At times, when public opinion is implacably against it, it takes courage to show love and compassion for those who do not conform.

In some cases our inner feelings are released as a result of an illness or trauma, or having a near death experience.

What happens when a person is regressed in order to find out about a previous life?
All knowledge of previous lives is locked away in the mind and NO ONE has access to it. On the occasions during sleep, when we communicate with our guardian angel and other spirit helpers, they impart all kinds of information to us. Some of this material is to be used by us in days to come, and is fed into the future subconscious part of the mind. However, they will sometimes tell us about their previous lives and even details of our own. This information is put into the past subconscious part of the mind, and for the most part remains undisclosed throughout our physical life.

A hypnotist attempting to bring out details of a person's previous life can only do so if Spirit allow it. They will then be given access to the information stored in their subject's past subconscious, but they will not know that this may refer to a previous life of the subject's spirit helper. There is nothing to be gained from the exercise except to stimulate interest in reincarnation.

When people in their *conscious* state think they are remembering a past life, it is also linked with whoever is with them from the Spirit World, impressing them with who they are, trying to get them to understand that they still exist maybe even wanting their help for one reason or another. The reason behind it will always be for positive good.

When someone is unable to speak, does this mean that there is something wrong with the mind?
No. The spirit is whole and never changes in that respect, so

there would be nothing wrong with the mind. However, in the case of someone unable to speak, it could be because their vocal cords, or a part of them essential to the speaking process is damaged. Or it could be that the brain itself is damaged (in the case of stroke victims, for instance) and although the brain is receiving the message from the mind, it is unable to act upon it.

Why do we dream?
Dreams are symbolic guidance to us from our spirit helpers. They put the message into the mind, which conveys it to the brain via the mind's eye. Thus it is there for us to remember and interpret.

What about repetitive dreams?
Dreams are repeated when an important message is just not getting through. There is the case of a friend of the author who had the same dream over several months.

In the dream his house was suffering from severe problems. Sometimes, there would be slates missing from the roof and sometimes the roof timbers would be rotten or broken with the sky visible through them. Another variation would see the water pipes leaking or water dripping down the walls. In the dream he would think to himself, " I must get a roofer/ plumber in." But of course when he awoke he would realise there was nothing wrong with his house.

After a period of time he realised there had to be a meaning to these persistent dreams and began to work out what it could be.

He knew that symbolically a house represents a person and the roof represents that person's natural protection.

This man, who at the time was in his 60s, worked in a physical job, was very busy both in work and in his leisure time too. What the dreams were telling him was that he was working too hard; he was becoming vulnerable, just like the house, to anything that might choose to invade him. The leaking water was showing him that his energy (water represents life) was draining away. Recognising the serious consequences if he did not slow down, he gave up some of his activities and took more rest. His health improved. The dreams ceased. The message from Spirit had been understood and acted upon.

What about those dreams that we do not remember?
They are not to be used at present and have been filed in a certain part of the mind, the sub-conscious future, ready for retrieval at the right time.

What is meant by astral or planet travel?
When we are asleep, there are times when our spirit leaves our body. It is a misconception to call it astral travel because when our spirit leaves our body at night it is usually to help someone on this planet. Very, very few are taken to the Astral Plane in sleep state, and then only for special reasons.

For the rest of us we leave our body in order to be given guidance by our spirit helpers or for us to give service to someone in need on our planet. This could take the form of comfort or healing, or to give help to those who are earthbound, giving them guidance to take away their fear. It could entail travelling to another part of the world – taken by our spirit helpers. Our spirit is still attached to our physical body by the silver cord however far we travel. At no time is our physical body in danger; it is protected by Spirit.

But please bear in mind that not everyone goes planet travelling, and it is very rare for anyone to be allowed to remember their journey upon waking.

Why do voodoo, curses and spells sometimes appear to work?
It is another case of autosuggestion, this time based on fear. The important factor is that the victim *knows* of the spell, otherwise it will not work. As long as the victim *believes* that the spell or charm will work, then it will, because of their ingrained belief in the practice. Thus the strength of their mind will overcome

common sense, for the mind is a very powerful tool.

Do not underestimate the power of the mind. It can make or break you. Positive thinking will destroy any fear within you and overcome any autosuggestion.

Questions and Answers on the Planet

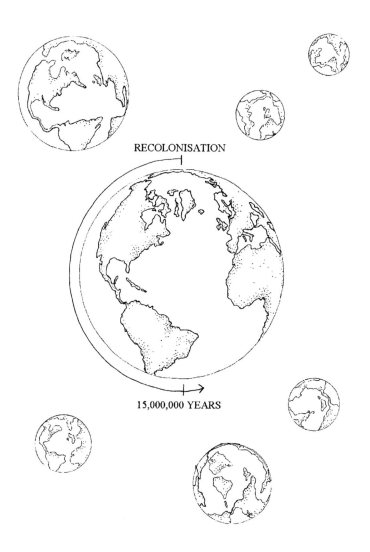

RECOLONISATION

15,000,000 YEARS

This section introduces a very controversial subject that many with a scientific interest or background will dispute. This information was given to the author direct from her spirit teachers and has been reproduced here. She has no knowledge of geology or the other subjects that would back up or argue against it. She only knows that Spirit would not lead anyone astray and that one day scientists will recognise the truth of it all. In the meantime it is for you to read and chew upon.

The origin of life on this planet is one of science's greatest mysteries. A number of theories are held by respected scientists, but the truth will never be known until science recognises the true nature of mankind and life itself.

While science remains ignorant of our true spirit nature, science will never have the true answer. In their search for an answer, scientists have put forward many suggestions that cannot actually be proved or clearly demonstrated. Everyone has a theory, but it will remain a theory because until mankind accepts that we are spirit, what our spirit is, how it exists in our physical body, and what happens when our physical body dies, they will never have the answer.

Many scientists believe that the evolution of life started from the sea. Some think it is linked with mineral deposits, granite etc. Many believe we evolved from an ape-like ancestor. But there are still a number of problems with these theories. They cannot accept the simple explanation that we are a spirit encased in a physical body, and were placed here as such from the beginning of human life on this planet.

***

How long has there been habitation on this planet?
This present colonisation began over fifteen million years ago. However, the earliest habitation of the planet goes back far, far beyond that.

Why is it that although scientists have discovered animal remains going back hundreds of millions of years, there have been only relatively recent human remains among their discoveries?
In the days when mankind first populated this planet, bodies were always cremated to complete the natural cycle – ashes to ashes and dust to dust. That which is of the earth will return to the earth.

Does the mention of this *present* colonisation mean that there has been more than one period of occupation?
Yes. There have been several periods of occupation other than the present one.

Why was there a need for re-colonisation?
This planet had exhausted certain resources and could no longer sustain life for animal and human occupation. The planet had to go through a process of regeneration, taking around two million years, to allow the vegetation of the planet to be replenished until it would be able to support substantial life again. Then there was the need to reintroduce human life.

But it takes hundreds of millions of years for resources such as coal and oil to be formed. Does the planet rest for that number of years?
No. The natural shift of landmasses, which takes place over many millions of years, exposes resources previously inaccessible. Once all these resources have been exhausted, this planet will no longer be used for human habitation.

How was it known when re-colonisation could take place?
Spirits from the Spirit World – we could call them scouts – working for the God power, knew that this planet was ready once again to receive intelligent life - mankind. So inhabitants of other planets that were spiritually and technologically advanced, were selected to come to this planet to live on it and take it forward in its evolution.

How were the planets selected?
The spirit scouts were aware of the different climates and temperatures on the earth and so selected inhabitants from planets that would suit the conditions on earth. In all, three planets were selected.

These planets had three different climates. It was necessary that the new inhabitants could easily acclimatise, thus the three planets from which they came were similar climatically to those weather conditions that they would meet on this planet at that time – very, very hot, very, very cold, and moderate.

The people who lived on the hot planet were black. The people living on the planet with the moderate temperature had yellow skins, and those living on the cold planet were white, and covered in hair from head to toe. You wouldn't find one person on this earth now who looks like the original male or female who populated it then. Time, and the mixing of races have changed all that.

Would it not have been easier to select people with the same colour skins?
No progression is made easy. The difference in people's colour is one of the main factors that mankind must learn to understand and accept. Black, yellow or white, mankind must learn to live in harmony, not because of the colour of their skin or appearance, but who they are within.

What about the Indians with red skin or those with a brown skin - where did they come from?
Their colour evolved from the mixing of the races.

What about the animals? Did they come from other planets too, and how did they get here?
Animals were brought in embryonic form by the colonists and preserved in conditions conducive to keeping them alive until such time as they arrived on the planet. With their highly advanced technology and scientific knowledge this wasn't a

problem. In the same way, edible plants were brought in the form of seeds, bulbs or spores to supplement the plants already here.

Were there any other plants and animals here before they arrived?
There was sparse plant life, fish and insects and a few different species that survived on the little that was available to sustain life.

But surely it would take light years for them to travel from other planets. How could they have carried out the re-colonisation?
With the limited technology we have today, it would not be possible to achieve. But the technology available on those planets millions of years ago was far in advance of anything we could even dream about now.

Why do we not have that technology now?
Over time many occupants of this planet became greedy, materialistic and unspiritual. Because of this they lost the ability to communicate with Spirit, and gradually lost their ability to use the technology.

Recent history has continued to provide similar examples. The philosophy and writings of the Ancient Greeks, the technology and organisation of the Roman Empire, the scientific advances of the Middle East were temporarily lost with the fall of the Roman Empire, and a dark age followed, which lasted for hundreds of years. During this time the invasions and depredations of various racial groups destroyed even more of the civilising influences that had existed.

It was not until some semblance of order had been restored in Europe that the slow recovery commenced with the Renaissance and has continued ever since with the last one hundred years providing scientific and technological advances originally undreamt of.

Will we ever regain that technology?
Once the people on this planet have regained the spirituality that once was here, and they can be trusted not to abuse the knowledge they have, the technology will be available again. In fact, the planet, although having a long way to go, is slowly beginning to lighten, and technological advances are being made at last.

What do you mean by saying the planet is beginning to lighten?
A planet is as dark or as light as the light (the spirituality) that shines from the people who live there. At present this is a very dark planet, but it is not the darkest. There are many planets that are much, much lighter than this one, as the spirituality of their population is far beyond that of the majority of people living here. However this planet is lighter than it once was, and during the Age of Aquarius it will see a great improvement as more and more people become aware of their spirituality, and of the need to look after others and the planet on which they live.

Can this planet go forward without the help of Spirit?
Those from the Spirit World work hard with us, impressing us with their wisdom, creativity and technology, and when working with our intuition they blend their knowledge with ours to take this planet forward.

We are nothing without Spirit, and Spirit say they are nothing without us; it is a partnership. When we look at what's around us, our technology, our buildings, our transport, our progress in healing techniques etc., they all evolved from thought, and those thoughts must have come from somewhere.

Of course we are quite capable of dealing with many aspects of our material lives using our own common sense and knowledge, but when we are really in need of help and are searching for an answer, this is when Spirit will offer advice. It is still up to us, using our free will whether we accept or not.

Has the planet changed since the re-colonisation?

As with all planets there have been great changes brought about by natural events. There have been great climatic changes; indeed the climate is changing now. There have been ice ages, floods, earthquakes, tidal waves, hurricanes, volcanic eruptions and soil erosion. Even in the short time that we have been keeping records we have seen changes, such as the disappearance and appearance of land.

Are there laws of the Spirit World that affect us on this planet?

Yes, there are. The principal law that applies is the need for us to love our neighbours. Should we hurt them in any way we will have to make retribution either here or when we return to the Spirit World.

It is our choice whether we observe or break our planetary laws, and if the latter, suffer the penalties. If we appear to "get away with it" then we may be required when we return to the Spirit World to deal with it then, if it breaks a law applicable there.

We must also remember we may infringe a moral code with no penalty being imposed whilst on the planet, but once again it may be contrary to the law of the Spirit World.

It is a paradox that the more sophisticated a civilisation becomes, the more laws are required to ensure its smooth running. Obviously laws concerning cars and drivers, payment of taxes etc. do not apply in the Spirit World. The laws required there are relatively few.

It is difficult for us to understand what a huge difference there is between life on a planet and life in the Spirit World. With the wonderful feeling of love around us, and the understanding that has been restored to us via the opening of our minds, it is extremely unlikely that we would even consider trying to break the laws of the Spirit World. They are literally unbreakable.

Are the actions of the environmentalists worthless if we are geared towards a world where resources will eventually be exhausted anyway?

Environmentalists play a big part in preserving this planet for as long as possible. They respect it, and work to help others to respect it too. We owe them a debt of gratitude, regardless of the fact that the time will come when the planet resources will be spent.

And there's more…

(Other questions you have always wanted to ask)

Who or what is God?

God is a power, a power that creates, a power that is the ultimate in love, a power that is within us all. The more love we have within, the more God power we have within us.

The idea has developed that God has the physical appearance of a man because it has been said that we are made in God's image, but this is not so. Our spirit incorporates, and is part of the God power. The spirit is then encased in a physical body for the duration of a physical life on a planet.

Some people think they have seen and spoken to God whereas they have been in communication with a spirit in service projecting an image of the physical form that they once occupied.

Is there such a thing as the devil?

The only devil that exists is the self we give in to in our weaker moments, when we exercise our free will and go along the pathway that our guardian angel is striving hard to prevent us taking. We all have the choice to do what is right, or to do what is wrong, and when we choose to go against our conscience then you might say we are giving in to the devil in us. But there is no such thing as the devil as a separate entity. The concept of the devil is just something invented by mankind to account for some people's weakness of will, or plain wickedness!

How can it be true that we are all sons of God?

We are not *sons* but *suns* of the God power. This means that everyone is a part of the God power and the light and the warmth that is emitted from us is as the warmth and light that is emitted from the sun. An individual can be described as a per-sun.

What does the God power want from us?
Throughout recorded history, mankind has taken it upon itself to act on behalf of the God power often with disastrous consequences. The incidences of religious wars, persecution, 'heretics' being burned at the stake and the Inquisition all bear this out. Even some more recent cases of 'ethnic cleansing' have had a religious basis.

The one thing in which the God power does need our assistance is for us to use the power of our love, and then many of the ills of this world would be cured and mankind could live in harmony.

The God power is the power of unconditional love, and we need have no fear of it. Additionally it does not require us to bow down and offer praise, for the God power does not have an ego that must be fed. It is we who need to recognise and overcome our own egos so that we can give our love and help to others.

Unfortunately, most of us have no idea why we were born onto this planet. The answer is simple; it provides us with many opportunities to further our spiritual growth, and we should be concentrating on this task.

There are many pathways to this goal, and if we could all accept this, then there would be no need to fight over what is the right (in our eyes) way to reach it.

No one has the right to claim that a country belongs to them; it is only in their care for a limited time. We came into the world with nothing material and will take nothing material away with us. However, when we leave we should be spiritually richer.

The God power is waiting for us to find out for ourselves that when we have love for each other, we will then achieve true peace and happiness.

Where was the God power when I was so much in need of it?
How many times have we heard this plea? How many times have we personally wished that a situation or problem could be removed from us by a 'divine hand'?

When natural disasters occur and thousands of people die, there appears to be neither rhyme nor reason for their deaths. How does this fit in with the divine plan? When people are in the throes of a trauma it is not easy to give them an explanation they can accept.

The answer is in two parts. Firstly, we have been given free will. Many of our problems are the result of exercising our free will. We have to accept that we must take responsibility for our actions and learn from our mistakes. Once people understand this, then the world will be a happier place.

Secondly, although we may not be aware of this, we have asked to come to this planet to further our spiritual growth. Choosing to do so includes taking the risks inherent in living on it.

The planet itself is evolving and earthquakes, floods and storms are a part of this process. Now mankind is adding to these problems with pollution, destruction of forests that provide our oxygen and reckless use of our finite resources. We cannot blame the God power for all of this; it is our free will combined with ignorance that exacerbates these problems.

Tragedies that we experience during our life here may contribute towards that which may be required to help us learn a lesson, or trigger a course of action, which will lead us onto our true pathway through this life. Many self-help groups, charities etc. have been started as the result of traumatic experiences.

We each have our guardian angel, walking beside us in this life, and they will try to impress upon our minds the best course of action to take. This may manifest as our conscience pricking us, intuition or a 'gut feeling'. However, should the trauma result in death, it may be that it is our time to go. We have reached the end of our allotted life span. It is also possible that we ourselves have contributed towards shortening our life.

The God power does seem at times to work in mysterious ways and with our limited knowledge we cannot always understand the motive behind this and may not do so until we return to our spiritual home.

Why does the God power allow people to get into positions of power if they are going to misuse it?
The simple answer to this is the same as that for many of the questions people ask. The God power has given us free will to think for ourselves. Considering the suffering that can ensue because of this, it might be considered a bad decision. But we do not want to be puppets, and how would we grow spiritually without free will and the problems we bring upon ourselves, with the opportunity to learn from them?

Although we do know that dictators and despots who bring suffering to their people will pay for it, either here or upon return to the Spirit World, for many this is of little comfort. It is only when we too return to the Spirit World, the fairness of the laws there will be apparent to us, and we will understand that there is compensation and retribution where appropriate, for all.

In a war situation where both sides are asking the God power to help them, how do those in the Spirit World deal with this dilemma?
Spirit will always endeavour to persuade both sides to try to settle their differences through diplomacy and negotiation. However, at this stage of mankind's spiritual evolution, wars seem to be inevitable. Those who instigate conflict for reasons of power, greed, national aspirations, ethnic cleansing, or the mistaken belief that their cause is just, have not learnt from history that right will always triumph in the end.

Because of their actions, thousands, sometimes millions of people will die, and of course those in the Spirit World are very distressed by this. So why don't they stop these conflicts?
It is because we have free will, that gift from the God power that is for us to use as we see fit. This gift is one of the God power's laws and those spirit helpers who try their utmost to impress upon us the best pathway to follow, have to stand back

when we don't listen to them and let us make our own mistakes, in the hope that one day we will eventually learn.

Similarly they cannot help by affecting the weather to help one side or the other, or by supplying any material advantages. However, regardless of what side the combatants are on, Spirit will always support those who are working for the good of others. In addition, what Spirit can do to ensure that right does triumph, and because they can see into the future, is to recruit highly evolved spirits to come to this planet, to be born into a physical body to lead the fight for peace and freedom.

We have all come to this planet to learn and to try to add to our spiritual growth. If we choose to do it the hard way, then that is up to us. We certainly take our physical life in our own hands when we ask to come to this planet.

What is prayer and does it work?
Prayer is a sincere and respectful communication between one person and Spirit. The thought, i.e. the prayer, is transmitted via their guardian angel to the appropriate spirit. There is always a reply, although it may not be the one we want. And there is always help although it may not be in the way that we wanted it - we may not even realise that our prayer was answered. Asking for material help, providing the motive is right, is an acceptable prayer to make. Prayer should be as simple as conducting a conversation.

A prayer for healing is always an acceptable prayer to make, and Spirit will do their utmost to help, but the result is not always as we would wish, as they must work within the confines of the physical body, and there are rules to which they must adhere.

Prayers that try to bargain are not acceptable. We should not need a 'favour' from Spirit in order for us to behave reasonably. Remember that we each have our pathway and although *we* can be responsible for moving from it, we cannot ask our spirit helpers to initiate that move. It is their responsibility to help us to remain on our pathway, however difficult that may be, and they cannot be a part of an attempt to by-pass it.

What is an angel?

An angel is a spirit working in service from the Astral Plane to help mankind. Angels do not have wings. They do not fly, they do not need to fly, as thought by us as they only have to think of being in a place and they have the power to be there. But they do have a wonderful spiritual light reflected from their spirit – their aura - and this has been seen and misinterpreted, and then misrepresented in religious paintings and literature. All spirits that are in service working from the Astral Plane with us here, are seen as angels.

Do we spend most of our time on a planet or in the Spirit World?

The Spirit World is our natural home where we have already spent, and will continue to spend, the majority of our eternal lives. The physical lifetimes we have in this and other planets are really only brief interludes in eternity.

We have the choice of how long we wish to remain on our spirit realm and whether to embark on another physical lifetime in order to have further experiences, which are not available on our realm.

Is it true that spiritual and earthly matters run side by side?

They certainly do. Our guardian angels are with us every minute of our waking moments and are aware of all that is going on in our lives, but they only intrude – or offer their advice – when they can see that what we are doing is going to make our lives more difficult, or that we could harm others or ourselves. They do not interfere with the everyday running of our lives, but their teachings and influences help us to deal with everyday problems in a spiritual way. Do not confuse this with consulting the Spirit World on every mundane decision you make.

Is there a difference between time experienced on the Earth and in the Spirit World?

Throughout the ages mankind has been ruled by time, nature's time. The natural rhythm of day and night, lunar months and the seasons, getting up at sunrise and retiring at sunset, it is the sun that ultimately influences our appreciation of time. Because there was no accurate way of measuring time, mankind became adept at using the sun (when it shone) to judge how the day was passing, and the growth of plants and trees to appreciate the seasons, and thus was closely attuned to nature.

In a sense, time is illusory. We all know how amazed we can be sometimes when it seems that time has flown, and when we are wishing it away it seems to drag.

When considering the effect of time in the Spirit World, it depends from which part of the world Spirit are working. Those working in service to us from the Astral Plane must conform to our concept of time here on earth.

The Spirit World does not have night and day, darkness and light as we do here. Their light is from a very different source from that which is received on the planet, and is not apportioned in the way we would recognise. Those in the spirit realms are still involved in plans. Thus there is a kind of time limit, but time is not as we understand it here - that is something we will only comprehend once we have returned to our realm.

What do we look like when we return to the Spirit World?

This question worries some people. Are we a lump of energy or a blob of light?

The simple answer is that we do not know. We do know that we will still be a spirit containing our soul and mind with all the knowledge and wisdom we have gained in our many lives. We also know that when people see Spirit they are dazzled by a bright light, unless the spirits concerned show themselves as they looked in their physical lives. Then they look the same as people we see around us.

Artists throughout the ages in the Christian world have

illustrated their feelings about this question. The God power is shown as an elderly gentleman infusing the spark of life into Adam. Angels with wings are shown among floating clouds, along with cherubs playing the harp. One thing they are sure about is that light is involved. Halos placed around the heads of the divine and holy figures show a light emanating from them.

We are aware that it is the spirit that gives out the light and energy. When asked to describe the appearance of a spirit our friends from the Spirit World have told us we would not understand, even if they tried to explain it. Of course we could turn around and say, "Try me." However, when we think how most of us would not understand if scientists of this world started to talk to us about quantum physics and sub atomic particles, then the comment from Spirit makes more sense to us.

As we feel perfectly normal and at home to be in a physical body while we are here on Earth, then no doubt we feel the same way about our appearance, whatever form it takes back home in the Spirit World.

If I have had more than one marriage, how is this resolved when I return to the Spirit World?
It all depends upon how the marriages ended. If love had lapsed then there would be no reason to meet. If not, then you need to appreciate that the Spirit World is a world of love, unencumbered by the needs and drives of a physical body. In addition to this, no one is allowed to impose himself upon another. Also, our attitude and understanding can change once our mind is unlocked, and we may see the relationships we had whilst on the planet in a different light once we return to the Spirit World.

While in a good loving marriage or physical relationship, it is easy to feel that this is the love above all, and that you would never wish to be parted from your loved one. But however beautiful and spiritual that love may be, it is a very different love from the one you share with your soul mate in the Spirit

World. Once back in the Spirit World with your mind unlocked, you will recognise the love you had for your physical partner as something very different, and although you may still have a love for each other it will not compare with that which you both have for your soul mates.

Will we be able to meet historical personages and famous people when we return to the Spirit World?
No, not in the way we may think. We certainly will not *see* their like again, for their body, which provides their outward appearance, is no more. However, they can still *project* the image of how they looked during their earthly life, and this may have led people to think we will have the same appearance for all time in the Spirit World. We must not lose sight of the fact that in the Spirit World we are spirit, with no need to assume the likeness of a physical body.

Can those from the Spirit World show themselves in the image of someone else i.e. a famous historical figure or a celebrity?
No. You can only assume the image of a person whom you have once been. It is the law of the Spirit World that you cannot project an image that was not yours – and the laws of the Spirit World cannot be broken.

Can we show ourselves as really old people even if our allotted life span only reaches middle age?
There would be no point in showing yourself in that way as the reason for showing yourself would be to be recognised, and no one would know you as an elderly person.

To show yourself as an old person would have no beneficial effect on anyone and thus it would not be an option.

Does the Spirit World see us as our physical form or as our spirit form?
Spirit sees us as we are at the time i.e. a spirit clothed in a

physical body. When the spirit healers are working on the physical body, it would be of no use to them to see only the spirit! At all times they are able to see our spiritual light ("By our light we are known)".

What does it mean, you are 'known by your light'?
When referring to your light it is the light reflected by your spirit within, the aura, and the brighter the light the more spiritual you are. Being "known by your light" means is that your spirituality is reflected for all to see and recognise.

You cannot hide your light from those in the Spirit World at any time, whether it is bright or dim.

Is it right to give 100 per cent of ourselves to others?
No. If you were to go through life giving 100 per cent of yourself you would lose your individuality. No one should expect it from you, and you shouldn't expect it from others.

A marriage, partnership, friendship, family etc. should at all times be built on a foundation of give and take - not wanting or giving all, but respecting and being respected.

Is it selfish to put yourself first?
No. It is neither selfish nor unspiritual; it is common sense. If you are constantly thinking of others and putting their needs before your own, the time will come when you have become so depleted by the calls on your time and energy that you will not be in a position to help anyone, and those whom you have tried to help will end up looking after you, only adding to the problems they already have to cope with in their lives.

'No' can be a healthy word if by saying it, and by putting yourself first you can conserve your health. Don't give of yourself to please others. By saying 'No' sometimes you can give others the opportunity to grow by giving them the chance to take on more responsibility, and to be less reliant on others.

How is it possible for our spirit to be drained?

Illness and great emotional upset can drain the spirit, but so too can looking after children, sick or elderly people. They can drain us of our energy, which in turn affects our physical body, and it is wise when you are feeling below par, and when you know you will be with them for any length of time, to send out a prayer asking for help in not giving any more of your power or energy than you can afford to give.

What is karma?

The word karma is man-made. Its meaning is this; whatever you sow in life, so too must you reap and if not in this life, then in the Spirit World. If you sow goodness, then you will reap goodness; if you sow destruction, then you will reap destruction; if you sow suffering for others then you must reap suffering for yourself. But this will not be in another physical life.

It seems unfair that there are people in this world who do no good at all and get away with it. Will they get away with it in the Spirit World?

No, nobody gets away with anything. If during their time on earth they make no effort to put right the wrongs they have done, then they will have to put them right when they return to the Spirit World. Unfortunately, it will be much harder then.

Having served a prison sentence for a serious crime that has resulted in a death or injury, does the perpetrator have to make further amends upon their return to the Spirit World?

The laws of the Spirit World ensure that no one escapes retribution for their wrongdoings. It will depend on what efforts have been made to atone for their act. If they have merely endured the sentence and have made no effort to atone, or have shown no remorse, then they will have to do all the work necessary to obtain forgiveness from their victim and for themselves, and make amends upon their return to their spirit realm.

If an effort has been made, and they are conscious of the great enormity of their crime and are deeply regretful, then there will be less for them to do, but forgiveness will still need to be sought and work carried out to help others as restitution for the mistakes they have made.

Why is the Spirit World opposed to capital punishment?
Capital punishment, or the execution of a wrongdoer, will in some cases result in the offenders choosing to be earthbound, and thus continuing their wickedness by suggesting and influencing – impressing – another of like mind, to do as they had done when in the physical body. If the offenders are imprisoned, then their guardian angels will have the opportunity to bring them to a better understanding of the wrong they have done. Having thus realised the error of their ways, they will be more willing to return to the Spirit World when it is their time to do so at physical death.

Do you always progress spiritually from your earthly life?
No. Some people return to the Spirit World less spiritual than when they arrived on the planet because of the type of life they have lived. When they look back on their life here, and realise the mistakes they have made, it will be a devastating blow. They will have to start regaining lost ground, which can take a very long time.

Do trees have a spirit?
Spirit is just another name for the life force, and everything that has a life has a life force. This includes not only animals, insects, birds and plants, but of course trees too. Without a life force, there is no life. When the tree comes to the end of its life, be it through natural decay or as a result of having been cut down, the life force is taken care of until it is needed to be placed back into a seed again to give it life. The care of the life

force of the tree is attended to by spirit gardeners.

Trees are very necessary to the planet as they provide oxygen for us to breathe, herbal medicinal remedies and food for us to eat. Considering the number of trees that are replaced each year, not to mention those in various stages of growth at any one time, it can be assumed that there is a large number of spirit helpers working hard to ensure the survival of this planet and its inhabitants.

Is it true that we start off as a plant and progress from there, becoming insects, animals etc. until we become human beings?
No, it is not true. The life force (spirit) that an animal, bird, fish, insect etc. would have is very different from that of a plant. Each living thing has the life force – or spirit – appropriate for them. The spirit does not change to accommodate the kind of being you are. Plants are always plants, animals are always animals and we, as humans, remain the same type of human life force throughout eternity.

What happens to animals after physical death?
They are taken to a part of the Spirit World that is especially for the spirits of animals, birds, fish, reptiles etc.

Does that mean that we will never see our pets again?
Not at all. When we leave our body at physical death, if the need is such, they will be there to greet us. Otherwise they will be there on the Astral Plane when we arrive. They can also visit us on the Earth Plane while we are still there to reassure us that they are fine, or to give us comfort. When we finally leave the Astral Plane to go on to our spirit realm, they will return to the animal kingdom, but if we wished to visit them there, we could do so.

Is it true that animals grow spiritually?
At one time people did not believe that animals had a spirit. We now know that without a spirit nothing can live. So does

their spirit incorporate a mind and soul? Over recent years, tales of how dolphins have helped people in distress, and how handicapped people swimming with dolphins have received healing and upliftment would certainly appear to show that these animals have a form of love for others.

When we think of dogs who have stayed by their injured masters, or have given help, dogs who help to guide the blind, dogs who are the ears of the deaf and who are taken into rest homes and hospitals, the PAT (Pets as Therapy) animal programmes, we see that pets do express a spiritual side, some even staying with and loving masters who are cruel and unkind to them.

Spiritual growth applies to all creatures great and small, and they all have the chance to grow spiritually in their own particular way.

How long is it before animals are reincarnated in a physical body after passing to the Spirit World?

Their lives and spiritual growth are far different from those of a human, and much less complicated. They can remain in the Spirit World for as long as is necessary but they do not have to wait as long as a human spirit waits before having the opportunity to have another physical life.

Have animals got psychic powers?

There have certainly been many cases where people have attributed the actions of their pets to a paranormal influence. Before being certain of this, we have to remember that animals in general have vastly superior senses of smell, hearing, eyesight, and awareness of body language than humans. Their world consists principally of the need to survive and feed. Their senses are geared to these objectives; they are not distracted in a way humans are by the material world. Thus many of the reactions we see as psychic are perfectly compatible with normal physical behaviour. However, there are no doubt instances when those in the Spirit World have impressed or guided animals in a way that has resulted in help which has saved human lives.

Should we speak to our children about death and dying?
We, as parents, should bring up our children to understand what this life is all about. This entails guiding them in the right direction and being an example for them to follow. We should show them how to be loving towards everyone, to show respect for each individual as well as respecting themselves. We should educate them about life, its ups and downs and the fact that coping with the downs helps them to learn. Death and dying are part of life's journey. This is a natural event with nothing to fear, and no great emphasis should be put upon it. It is only the death of the physical body and a further step for our spirit when it returns to the Spirit World.

How does Spirit view euthanasia in a case where suffering has become too much to bear?
Everyone has an allotted life span that has been calculated to take account of the pathway they have planned to take and no one has the right to shorten that. However, when someone has had more pain and suffering than they can bear, Spirit understands how someone close to them could be driven to end that person's agony, because it is action taken out of a love and care for the sufferer. Motive is the all-important factor in such a case.

Does the Spirit World make allowances for those with illnesses or disabilities and their ability to cope with life, when considering the cases of those who have committed suicide?
Those in the Spirit World *never* judge. They are love - understanding and compassionate - and know the suffering and trials and tribulations each person has endured in their life. We alone judge our actions, and should we find we could no longer face life and end it ourselves, no one will judge us but ourselves. We would know why we took such action, and

we may be a little disappointed with ourselves, but we would also know the circumstances and be advised to judge ourselves accordingly.

Is it true that someone receiving a blood transfusion or transplant of any kind will take on part of the donor's characteristics?
Blood, the heart, lungs etc. are of the physical body, and as such can be transferred to another physical body but *no part* of anyone's spirit – or characteristics - can be transferred to anyone else. Your spirit and characteristics are yours and yours alone; they are whole and will always remain so.

A misconception may have occurred from stories told by recipients of donor organs who have *appeared* to take on interests or characteristics of the donor. What has in fact happened is that the donor, now in the Spirit World, and interested in the person who received their organ, has drawn close to that person. For a brief time only they have impressed the recipient with a little of the personal details they had while in a physical body. This is a temporary situation only and donors will soon move away to continue with their own lives in the Spirit World.

Is it possible to preserve a dead body by using cryogenics in order to bring it back to life in the future?
Some people believe that after death caused by a disease, or a medical condition untreatable by our present knowledge, it is possible to preserve the body by deep-freezing (cryogenics). They think that when, at some time in the future it is possible to treat the condition, the body can then be thawed, brought back to life and given the appropriate treatment.

What they do not appreciate is that at the time of death the spirit leaves the body. Even if it were possible to thaw the body successfully, there will be no spirit to energise it and they will be left with a body. It will not be 'alive' as we are; there will be no spirit - mind or soul - there.

Are all fingerprints unique or are there others the same?
There are identical fingerprints on others, but to find them would
be like looking for a needle in a haystack. However, there are no
two lights the same. By this we mean the aura surrounding each
person, the light shining out from their spirit, which identifies
them, and there is no like in either a physical world or in the
Spirit World.

Is there such a thing as a ghost?
Yes, there certainly is. But let us ask another question – what
exactly do we mean when we talk about a ghost?

What kind of image does it conjure up? Is it a headless corpse
carrying its hapless head under its arm, or perhaps something
white and formless with flapping arms and dark eyes glowing?
Certainly, it has to be something that frightens. Surely that is
the definition of a ghost, isn't it?

But why must the concept of a ghost be of something that
instils fear? Could it be, that like so many things, it is born out
of fear of the unknown? However, once a fear is faced, once
the mystery is unmasked, it loses all power to frighten. So let
us explore further to unmask this mystery. Let us ask another
question:

What *is* a ghost?
We know that ghosts exist, but not in the way that is popularly
understood. Using another word may help to enlighten us. Let
us use the word 'spirit' – for ghost is only an old name for
spirit.

What is a spirit?
A spirit is you or me. We consist of a spirit that has within it
two main components, a soul and a mind which, at this present
time is clothed in a physical body, either that of a male or a
female. When the physical body dies, the spirit leaves and
goes to another place. From that place, a number of spirits
are allowed to travel back to the Earth in order to be of service

to the people living there. They have great power when they return, a power far greater than they ever had while occupying a physical body, but this power can only be used in love, to help in whatever way they can. It cannot be used to hurt anyone.

So what of those tales of hauntings and other such scary stories?

If a spirit wishes to communicate with someone they love who is still here on Earth, they need to show themselves in the form their loved one would recognise. In order to do this, they use the power of their mind to superimpose the image of the person they were, on to their spirit form. In this way their loved one will be able to see and know them.

Wouldn't it be a shock to the bereaved one?

Indeed it could be a shock to a grieving loved one to suddenly see the one they have lost in front of them, especially if they do not believe in a life after death. And this is how the stories of ghosts have emerged. An action born of love has been so misunderstood that it has instilled a fear in the one person they wanted to love and reassure.

Once spirits understand the effect their appearance has had on their loved one, they may withdraw. This does not mean they are no longer there, for they will be close on hand to help in whatever way they can. But if they need to convey a vital message to the one they have left behind, then they may appear again, not to frighten, but to prompt them to either conquer their fear and attempt to communicate, or ask someone to do the communicating for them.

"Ghost" is another word for spirit, and where a spirit appears, so too does love.

What is an earthbound spirit?

An earthbound spirit is quite simply a spirit who has not yet returned to the Spirit World, who has for one reason or another, opted to remain on the earth. There are many reasons for them to do so but once they understand what happens if they return to the Spirit World then they do not linger.

What is a low earthbound spirit?
Rather than 'low' shall we say a mischievous spirit? They are troublesome earthbound spirits who are intent on mischief. However, having left their physical body, they have even less power than they had when in that body so they aim to use the power belonging to someone who is still in the physical body by trying to persuade them to make mischief!

How are earthbound spirits able to communicate with us?
Although an earthbound spirit has not the power to move objects in a way a spirit from the Astral Plane can, they are able to communicate their thoughts to someone of like mind. This they do by using their sixth sense, which is the only sense they now have. This ability is open to all of us here, but is seldom used to its full potential because we have the other five physical senses at our disposal. The hustle and bustle of 'civilisation' also distracts our minds from an ability that was once a natural sense to use.

Can *anyone* be influenced by an earthbound spirit?
Each of us has an inner light reflecting our inner goodness. The more spiritual we are, the brighter the light. Those who have such a dim light that these mischievous spirits can influence them are of a very low moral character, and they are unlikely to be reading this! They are the sort of people who would need no encouragement to make mischief or even to do harm in one way or another. Someone who is basically good would repel such spirits by that very goodness. We are not talking about saints or angels, only the like of you and me!

They can draw close to someone who is of like mind i.e. who thinks and acts along the same lines as they do, and they put ideas or suggestions into their mind. Earthbound spirits cannot do anything physical so they get someone else to do their dirty work for them! However, other evolved spirits work very hard to persuade such spirits to leave the earth and cease their mischief.

Can earthbound mischievous spirits return to Earth once they have left it?

A spirit who has caused serious problems, upsets or any kind of deep hurt while on the Earth has forfeited the right to return to earth as a spirit helper in the foreseeable future. They will not be considered for any service on Earth, but will be returned to the spirit realm from which they have come. From there they will have to earn the forgiveness of everyone they have hurt.

How does the Spirit World promote understanding of Spirit to cynical earthbound people?

Those spirits who are earthbound, and who had a cynical attitude to life when in a physical body may well view the Spirit World in the same light. Spirit would not have an easy task to change their jaded point of view, but over time, Spirit's determination and the unfailing love that is brought to the task, will persuade the earthbound spirit to give the Spirit World a try!

Is it true that you can be possessed by a spirit?

No spirit can possess you. A spirit may impress your mind, but it is impossible for any spirit to occupy your body. It's *your* body and *yours* alone.

We have been taught that when spirits come closer to us to impress us, what actually happens is that they move closer into our aura, *their* mind coming closer to our *mind.* This they can achieve if their light is of the same brightness as ours. If your light is dim or dark, you attract someone with the same light; if your light is warm and bright you attract someone whose light is warm and bright too. So at all times, it is *light* attracting *light* or *like* attracting *like.*

If you are in control of the quality of your thoughts, they are not negative, bitter, angry etc. your light remains warm and bright. When you allow others to upset you, and you become quick to anger, are revengeful or destructive, then your light dims and you are left in the dark. You are then attractive to those who are earthbound and who are of the same nature. They can draw closer, and will enjoy sharing your company.

Remember that it is the quality of your thoughts and deeds that will protect you and take you forward on your spiritual pathway.

Then if it is true that a spirit cannot enter your body, what happens when someone speaks in trance?
The spirit comes close into the aura of the communicator, channelling their words through the communicator's voice box.

What is a poltergeist?
One thing that a poltergeist is *not* is an earthbound spirit! A poltergeist is a spirit who has been allowed to return to earth in service and when they move or even throw things around, this is not to frighten but to enlighten, and to attract attention. They would not hurt anyone and could not do so. Neither do they wish to frighten, but sometimes it is the only way to draw attention to a person, object or problem. As with all spirits who return to the earth, they have come in love. Tales of physical harm have been the result of reports that have been distorted, misunderstood or greatly exaggerated!

What should we do if we see a ghost – or spirit?
Give them your love. With the combination of your love and their power what a lot of good you can do together!

Is it possible for anyone to bring a spirit back to Earth in order to communicate with them?
No. Communication is entirely under the direction of the Spirit World. It may also be that the spirit does not wish to communicate because of what happened whilst they were in

a physical body. Additionally, it is not as easy as picking up a telephone. The mechanics of communication are not simple, and have to be learned. If the spirits have gone back to their realm, then there is no way a link can be made. There is also the possibility that the spirit is now working as a guardian angel and must remain with their charge at all times.

Then again the spirit could be communicating with someone without their realising it, especially if there is no one to act as a communicator. A song may come into their mind that they cannot get rid of; this is Spirit giving them a message via the words of the song. They may smell perfume, aftershave or pipe tobacco, see that pictures have moved or experience other phenomena. In these cases it is the link of love which has brought them together and not a demand for their return. We cannot command or demand to see a loved one who has returned to the world of Spirit.

What factors influence Spirit to move things to attract attention?
You are referring to the practice of spirits in service to the planet physically moving articles to attract the attention of someone who needs to be made aware of something. The moving of a picture or photograph is sometimes used by those who have passed out of their physical body to tell their loved ones that they are there, and that they are fine.

What is ectoplasm?
Ectoplasm is a substance that comes from the spirit and it needs those in a physical body in conjunction with those from the Spirit World to make it.
It is used by Spirit in healing and in physical mediumship, and when seen it looks like dry ice or a white, smoky haze. When used for physical mediumship and healing, it helps to solidify whatever is being built up by Spirit, and is something that people, including scientists, are at present unable to understand.

What is a 'near death experience'?

A 'near death experience' is when the spirit leaves the body, at a time in the physical life when that body is close to death. The spirit leaves the body, but the cord has not been cut so the person is still alive. The spirit then returns to the body and physical life is resumed. This is because it is not their time to go; they have not reached their allotted life span, and although it is possible to leave the physical life before the life span has been reached, there is a reason for them to remain. It may be that they have been given the privilege to enlighten others, to tell them that death is not to be feared and that there is life *after* death; to tell them that death is only the ending of a *physical* life and that their spirit lives on.

Many who have had this experience have found that it has changed their lives completely. They see everything in a different perspective and they no longer have a fear of dying.

What is an 'out of body experience'?

In an 'out of body experience' or a 'near death experience' the spirit actually leaves the physical body for a short time, but the silver cord remains intact so that the spirit can return to the body at a moment's notice.

A near death experience is as a result of a severe illness, the trauma of a road accident or of anything that brings a person close to physical death. There have been reports of people witnessing their own operation from a point near the ceiling, while their body lay beneath them on the operating table. It has also been known to occur as someone lies dangerously ill in bed.

People's accounts are similar in many ways. Many report being taken to a beautiful place, sometimes meeting members of their family; others talk of crossing water but they each describe the beauty of the place to which they are taken as 'out of this world'. In all cases the people who have had these experiences lose any fear of death that they may have had in the past.

As opposed to a 'near death experience', an 'out of body

experience' can occur at any time. A woman has told of seeing her husband standing beside her, and yet at the same time she could see him asleep in his chair. Another tale has been told of someone ill in bed seeing beside her the person who has been giving the patient healing. They later discovered that at that time the healer had been home asleep in bed.

One lady reports how after having an argument with her daughter she lay in her bed, tossing and turning, unable to sleep. As she lay there she saw her daughter approach her bed, mouth the words "I'm sorry," and then back away from the bed and disappear through the wall!

Another account is given by a mother about her son, who called out to her from his bedroom on two consecutive nights. He begged her to tell his friend's grandfather to leave his room. It appeared that he could see the friend's grandfather, who was a healer, there in his bedroom, whereas the gentleman in question was at home asleep in his own bedroom. There are countless tales of experiences of a similar or very different nature, but all occurring when the 'traveller' is known to be asleep.

Although people having an 'out of body experience' often describe it in the same way as those who have had a 'near death experience', some people have reported having quite frightening or distressing experiences. Unknown to them, Spirit have tailored the experience to their need. There could be many reasons for these disturbing incidents but one could be to deter someone who is thinking of ending their physical life. It is another way of communicating with them and often results in a change for the better in their approach to life and the way they live it. Once again, it is Spirit showing that a physical life is a temporary experience, whilst our life as a spirit is continuous.

What is the sixth sense?
Many are not aware that we use our sixth sense constantly in our everyday lives. We all know about the five physical senses - sight, hearing, smell, taste and touch - but the sixth sense is

not a physical sense and is therefore not so easily recognised. This is the sense we use almost unconsciously; we get a 'hunch' about something, a feeling that we can't explain, an impression, intuition, premonition. This is the sixth sense, and the sixth sense is of the spirit, not the body.

Has extra-sensory perception any connection with Spirit?

Extra-sensory perception, or ESP. as it is commonly known, has been defined as the supposed ability of certain individuals to obtain information without the use of normal sensory channels.

The particular aspect of ESP that has intrigued scientists and layman alike, is the possibility of mind-reading, or the transmission of information from one person's mind to another. Thousands of experiments have been carried out to determine this ability. Of course there is always the element of chance that one person will guess what another is thinking, but the evidence is inconclusive.

Where scientists do believe that there is some evidence of this happening is in the case of identical twins, where if one is ill or suffers a trauma, it is not uncommon for the sibling to be aware of this. With twins there is obviously a very strong physical bond and generally they are likely to spend more time together than many children. This also applies to their guardian angels, and it is they who communicate information to each other and then to the twin.

It is also felt that where people have premonitions of disasters, often in dreams, this is also a case for a belief in ESP. Once again it is their guardian angel or spirit helpers who are giving them the information in their dreams.

Only Spirit are able to pass knowledge from one person's mind to another, and this is only done if it is appropriate to do so. They do this to make us think, to be aware that there are other things happening of which our normal senses may be unaware, and to make us realise we have more than a physical existence.

In the case of those who seek paranormal experiences, is Spirit willing to assist at all times?
Spirit are always willing to help to enlighten others to the existence of the Spirit World and will cooperate when, if by doing so, this would be achieved. However, Spirit would not be a party to something borne out of a wish to sensationalise or frighten or anything that would have an unspiritual outcome.

Why is it that some people are able to see auras and hear spirit voices?
We are all at different stages of spiritual evolvement, and the gifts we are given to us by Spirit are appropriate to that evolvement. Should we not have these gifts it does not mean we are unevolved, but that our work here is following a different pathway. It is unfortunate that some people who have these gifts do not develop them in a way that will be of help to others. Because of this, the message or information they give to others is often at a basic or psychic level, and is misinterpreted by them. They will then have unwittingly committed a disservice to mankind.

What is the difference between psychic and spiritual?
Everyone here on the planet has the ability to be psychic, but even so, they must be taught how to use it in a spiritual way. Those working with the psychic without training are working at a lower level. It is necessary for them to develop their spiritual senses, and then combine them with their psychic ability in order for them to make full and proper use of their gift. When the two are blended, the level of work will be lifted to the extent that people can benefit from being given spiritual guidance. Developing spiritual awareness creates the ability to understand messages that have a symbolic meaning. Remember that when interpreting such messages, you are personally responsible for ensuring that they are accurate.

Beware of people who call themselves psychics and have not trained to become spiritually aware. A lot of damage can be caused by the wrong interpretation of messages from Spirit. It is the law of the Spirit World that Spirit never, ever give a negative message; their communication always steers in a positive direction, showing the positive way to go, the positive way of looking at a situation. So be very suspicious if you are given a message that can only be described as negative. Spirit only bring upliftment, help and hope. If your message does not bring any of these, then do not accept it!

Does the Spirit World have control of the way in which healers and clairvoyants use their gifts?

Everyone has the potential to give spiritual help to others in one way or another. Those who work as healers, or use a gift of clairvoyance to help others, will have spiritual helpers in addition to their guardian angel, and they will know what is happening at all times. Each person should have their own personal code of conduct and have a responsibility to keep within those boundaries. There is no need to 'keep a check' as each person will have their individual support and advice from their own spirit helpers. Spirit does not control, as both disciplines are allowed to make their own mistakes, and thus to learn.

If these gifts are not going to be used correctly, why does Spirit give them to these people?

Spirit uses as many avenues or channels as possible in an attempt to awaken us to Spirit. It is a many-pronged attack on the general lack of spiritual awareness on this planet. There is always the hope that a chance contact (spirit arranged), will lead people to a place where they can receive proper training and are then able to make full use of their gifts.

Why do some communicators – or mediums - use psychometry when communicating with Spirit?

By holding a personal item given to them by another person – usually a watch or ring – communicators will give a spirit reading or message, and this method of working is known as psychometry. The theory is that a personal item retains something of the spirit or psyche of a previous owner.

However, trained mediums, who have their awareness of Spirit and understand how to interpret the meaning of symbols, can work without using props or gimmicks such as personal items, flowers or coloured ribbons. These items do not retain or absorb any part of a person's psyche. The information provided by the medium comes from Spirit and from no physical source.

Why do some people use ouija boards, tarot cards and crystal balls etc to communicate with Spirit?

Some people feel they need this kind of tool in order to communicate with Spirit when in fact all they have to do is develop their sensitivity to Spirit and learn to communicate one to one with them. A medium – and we can all be mediums in our own right – does not need such accessories. These tools are often used by psychics or beginners and often the message is interpreted purely on a psychic level rather than the deeper, spiritual level.

What place does television have in promoting the understanding of Spirit? Are there ethical dilemmas that may arise from using this medium?

Television is part of the modern world, and Spirit is part of everything in this world. There is no reason why television should not play a part in helping to broadcast the understanding of Spirit. There are unfortunately unscrupulous people in all walks of life and there are those who would use their spiritual gifts to take advantage of others, whether on a one-to-one basis or on a television network. But be assured that Spirit - and those working for Spirit in a physical body – work hard to ensure these people are identified for what they are, and limit the harm that they could do.

It is said that there is no bad publicity, and if this stirs an interest in Spirit, that interest can be directed to those who can help and enlighten.

Do Spirit need to rest?
Yes. As we need our sleep and rest when we are tired physically, mentally and emotionally, Spirit when working with us from the Astral Plane also get tired, not physically because they no longer carry their physical body, but mentally and emotionally. So they need to rest to replenish their energy for as long as it is needed for them to recharge themselves.

We must remember that working with mankind is not an easy task. What they see and deal with can still affect them emotionally and mentally. Just because they are pure spirit and have tremendous power they are still sensitive to what they are working with here on this planet when in service to us.

And there's more……. there's always more.

Questions and Answers on the Chakras

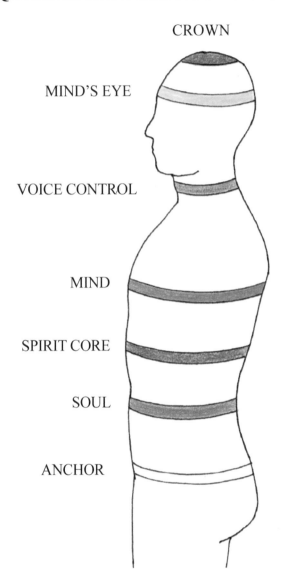

CROWN

MIND'S EYE

VOICE CONTROL

MIND

SPIRIT CORE

SOUL

ANCHOR

What is a chakra?

A chakra is a power or energy point, where power flows to and from the spirit.

Where does the power come from and where does it go?

The power comes from your spirit and is fed to the physical body. When we are working with those from the Spirit World they can supplement our energy if required. In addition to this, we also unknowingly pick up energy from other people and the cosmic energy that energises this planet.

How many chakras - or power points - are there?

There are many chakras but seven main ones.

Where are they?

They are of the spirit but their location in relation to the physical body is as follows:

     the crown
     the middle of the forehead
     the throat
     the chest
     under the rib cage – the solar plexus
     the abdomen
     the base of the spine

What is each chakra's function?

The crown chakra is the place where power enters the spirit when healing of the physical body takes place. If the spirit is depleted then it is necessary for this chakra to be opened up so that healing power can be poured through into the spirit first before healing of the physical body can commence.

The chakra located in the area of the middle of the forehead is working with the minds eye. When messages are sent from the mind to the brain via the mind's eye then this chakra will be supplying the power. When working with Spirit mind to mind, this chakra is opened further as more power is required.

The chakra that is situated in the area of the throat comes into use when speech is an important factor in the service in which we are involved at the time.

The chakra often referred to as the heart chakra because of its proximity to the heart comes into use when working mind to mind with Spirit.

The chakra that is in the area known as the solar plexus is what is known as the core because it is the link between the mind and the soul when working together and each message passes through it.

The chakra in the abdominal area is of course working with the soul.

The final chakra, which is at the base of the spine, is known as the anchor. It is here that the silver cord attaches the spirit to the physical body and it is here that most of the power is stored.

Is it true that the chakras have to be opened in order for Spirit to work with mankind?

All except the crown chakra are open during our waking hours. Only the crown chakra remains closed because it is only required when the spirit is being healed and in this event, Spirit will open and close it.

The chakras open further when working with Spirit and remain so unless we make a positive effort to return them to their usual position. To do this it is necessary to envisage yourself descending a very tall, spiral staircase – imagining a very high tower would be ideal. You need to imagine coming down slowly, step by step, around and around in a spiral like a coil closing up until you reach the bottom. If your mind is still racing, it is necessary to do it again until you feel you are 'grounded'. Using a coil or spiral staircase in this exercise helps to ensure that the process too, affects the chakras that are situated not only at the front, but also at the back of the spirit. If you do not do this, you may find that your mind is too alert, things keep going round and round in your mind and you cannot relax.

There will come a time in your progression when your chakras will open and close quite naturally.

Do chakras have colours?
No, power is colourless and is not visible to the naked eye. However, there are symbolic colours associated with each chakra as a means of indicating their purpose:

The crown chakra is symbolised in the colour purple because healing is such a spiritual function.

The mind's eye chakra is shown as yellow because thinking positively is an important factor when working with the mind.

The throat chakra is represented by that dark muddy green that we know shows negativity. When first working consciously with Spirit using speech, it is quite natural to feel negative, lacking a belief in our ability to be a communicator for Spirit and thinking that the words that we speak are our own. Because of this, our negative attitude is symbolised in that dark, negative green.

The chakra known as the heart chakra is symbolised in the colour orange, which represents wisdom. When working with Spirit mind to mind to help others, the wisdom that has accumulated during this lifetime comes to the fore and is used in service.

The core chakra is lavender, a pastel form of purple, symbolising the sensitivity and spirituality of its role.

The soul chakra is red, for although we know that controlled emotions are represented by pink, more often it is the raw emotion, the one that we have not yet managed to control, that will be the one that surfaces.

The anchor chakra is symbolised by white, which represents balance, as it is here that the balance of power is controlled.

Questions and Answers on Aura Colours

While we are in a physical body we are unable to see our spirit, although the field of light and energy it generates, the aura, can be visible at times.

The aura can be seen as a continually changing halo of colour, generally around the head, body, arms and hands. The colours reflect thoughts and emotions, what a person is thinking and feeling at the time it is seen. As the thoughts and feelings change, so too do the colours reflected in the aura. On the occasions we are privileged to see the aura, it is with our mind's eye not the physical eye, and if we attempt to look at it with the physical eye we cannot see it at all!

Every living thing has an aura. That is one manifestation of the spirit which can be proven scientifically, as auras can be photographed by a special camera. The aura pattern is unique to each person and identifies each one as an individual. No two auras are the same, as they reflect the mind and soul growth that is different for everyone.

Because people here did not understand how those from the Spirit World were able to travel from there to this planet, the shimmering ever-changing appearance of the aura was interpreted as wings, and this is why painters of religious subjects showed spirits (angels) with wings and halos.

Not everyone is fortunate enough to see an aura. It is entirely up to Spirit whether or not they are allowed to do so, and then only for a special reason. It is quite common to be shown only part of the aura emanating from just one part of the body, such as the hand when someone is using it to emphasise a point.

Some people may have seen an aura without realising it, putting it down to a trick of the light or a problem with their eyesight. If Spirit is using this method to get someone's attention, then no doubt they will continue to give them the experience until the message is understood.

The meaning of each different colour has been given straight from our spirit teachers, who have been questioned and questioned in order that we are clear on every point, and they have made corrections where necessary. The message of the aura colours is a universal language, on this planet and in the Spirit World.

How many aura colours are there?

There are eleven aura colours, ten of which continue with us into the Spirit World; the eleventh, brown, relates to material things and has no place there.

What are the other aura colours?

Yellow, dark muddy green, lime green, orange, peach, red, pink, white, blue and purple.

Can more than one colour be seen in the aura at any one time?

Most certainly. More often than not we have a mixture of thoughts and feelings, and these will, of course, be reflected in the number of colours in the aura.

How long does a colour show in the aura?

It is there for as long as the thought and feeling that it reflects is with that person. Someone who is very negative is not going to change that in a moment and therefore the dark, muddy green will be with them for quite a time. That is not to say that other colours will not appear alongside it. Red may appear and disappear just as quickly as a person flares up in anger and then calms down again.

What do each of the aura colours represent and how is this shown?

Each aura colour has a different meaning as shown overleaf.

YELLOW

Yellow reflects a positive attitude to life, of thinking in a positive way and having positive feelings about a situation. This manifests itself when confronting problems. Instead of letting the issue get the upper hand, someone showing yellow in their aura would have a more balanced way of looking at it, putting it into perspective, seeing the pluses and not being weighed down by the negative aspects.

Those with yellow in their aura would be optimistic and have a more open-minded attitude to life. This would be reflected in their general health, because a generally cheerful and positive outlook is conducive to better physical wellbeing. A positive attitude is infectious and affects those around them. As a result the atmosphere is lifted, and people are attracted to their side.

DARK, MUDDY GREEN

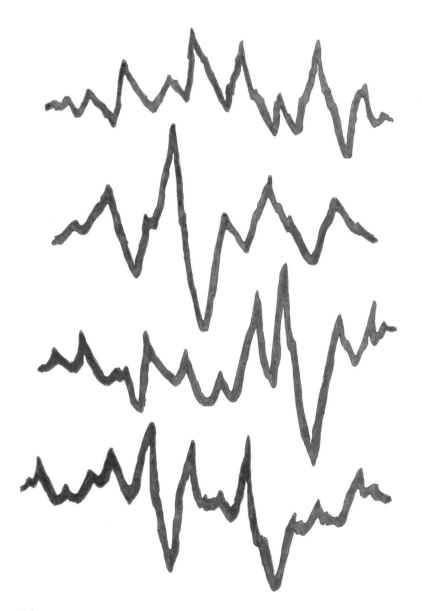

This is the opposite of yellow because it reflects negative thoughts and feelings, and has a sobering and depressing effect on those coming into contact with it. This colour reflects low self esteem, lack of confidence and an attitude that encompasses an unwillingness to even try. 'Can't', 'couldn't', 'daren't' are attitudes that bear that out.

Unfortunately this negativity will bring a person down, and those around them. It seems to be part of a vicious circle that is difficult to break. Once someone has lost faith in himself, he tends to lose faith in everything, feel insecure and pessimistic about life itself. The worry and despair that sometimes accommodates this thinking can also adversely affect their health.

Once people can start to look at things in a more positive way, bring yellow into their thinking and feeling, they will be surprised how much better they will feel - happier and healthier.

LIME GREEN

Lime green is indicative of a person who at the time is working with, and s - t - r - e - t - c - h – i - n - g the mind. This does not include the mundane, everyday thoughts that accommodate every day living but those in which you have to think hard, concentrate, or let your mind explore.

Solving a difficult problem, creativity such as writing, painting, designing, composing, planning and calculating are all activities that bring lime green into the aura. When meditating, or working with Spirit when the mind is being used, lime green will be there in the aura.

ORANGE

Orange is the colour that reflects wisdom. Wisdom, as opposed to knowledge, is attained by learning from life's experiences. A person could live to be a ripe old age and still have very little wisdom because, no matter what experiences they have had and everyone has the opportunity in life to learn, they did not learn from them. You can have a child, who in its short life has experienced things that many do not even know of, and who has learned so much from these experiences that he can teach his parents – a case of a wise head on young shoulders.

But of course, no matter how wise a person has become, the colour of orange in the aura is only apparent when using that wisdom. The image of a wise old man or a wise woman is associated with goodness, but this is not necessarily so as anyone can learn from life's lessons, and the wisdom is not always used to benefit mankind.

PEACH

Peach is the natural progression from orange, as it represents teaching. Throughout life we learn from many different people in many different walks of life. From parents we learn basic skills such as how to tie shoelaces and to feed ourselves, etc. We learn how to read and write from teachers. Our siblings and friends teach us things that help us to be accepted in our peer group. A petty thief sent to prison or a detention centre could learn from other inmates how to avoid getting caught next time! We also learn from the good examples set by decent people.

But when we are learning all these lessons, would peach be showing in the aura of those from whom we are learning? Possibly not. This is because peach represents teaching with love, wisdom and spirituality in order to help others in a way that would aid their spiritual progression. The motive to help others is an important factor and it must be recognised that without this, peach would not appear in the aura at all.

Brown and material thoughts go hand in hand while we are on the planet but once we are in the Spirit World and have had our minds unlocked, then brown will have no place there except when working from the Astral Plane with us, and helping us to deal with a material problem.

To have brown in the aura indicates only that you are thinking about and consequently having some feelings about a material issue. It does not mean you are materialistic. It simply means that, like everyone else on the planet, you have concerns about your survival here. We all have to think about the food we eat, the roof over our head and the money to provide both. There can be times when worries about this are all encompassing and we can think of nothing else. Naturally, brown would be the predominant colour in our aura at such a time.

That is not to say that we should not try to balance it by looking at the broader issue, getting it into perspective – assuming, of course that we are not penniless, starving, and/or homeless.

When we have a shopping spree and are treating ourselves, then brown will be the prominent colour in our aura. However, if we thought of nothing else but our material possessions, that would be a problem indeed. Similarly the millionaire whose life's work is to make money will frequently display brown in his aura. If his life did not go beyond that, then that would be a sorry tale indeed. But suppose he uses that money to help others? Then there would be many other colours in the aura and his life would be more than fulfilled.

All we have to do is to try to balance our material thoughts and feelings with our spiritual, and there will be a balance of colours in our aura too.

RED

Red is for danger - the danger that comes from letting our emotions get out of control. The gamut of emotions is quite extensive when you think of love and hatred, and everything in between. When these emotions are with us day in and day out they can wear us out! They can take over our lives and consequently our health. And that's dangerous!

But how could love be a danger to anyone? Surely love is all goodness? This is not necessarily true. The smothering love that is possessive, the selfish love, and the love that begets jealousy are not born out of goodness. This kind of love can only harm the lover and the loved alike

Another emotion that is common in so many compassionate people is the kind-heartedness that takes on others' problems to the detriment of their own health and wellbeing. Decisions made with the soul, where common sense and reasoning is overpowered by overwhelming love and compassion, is as harmful as any other raw emotion that has not been brought under control. Even love and compassion must be controlled so that the heart does not rule the head. Without this control we are oversensitive, taking offence where none was intended. We need to learn to step back from a situation in order to see it in perspective, without losing our capacity to care.

Jealousy, vindictiveness, a wish for revenge, spitefulness, anger, bitterness, hatred and those many other negative emotions only serve to harm us and can be self destructive.

Yet we all have the power to change that red in our aura just by exercising a little control.

Showing love in an unselfish way, giving loved ones the freedom to love us in their own way, in their own time, will reap its own reward,when the love is wholeheartedly returned!

Turning jealousy to good use - using envy of another's ability or possessions to spur us on to achieve rewards in our own field of excellence can have a really positive outcome from something that could have served us ill. When another's appearance makes us a little green-eyed monster, we should compliment them. Our compliment will give them pleasure, and by giving pleasure we will feel the benefit.

When anger seems to consume us, we must channel it. If someone or something raises our ire, then we should use the energy we have spent on this anger by doing something about it! Reason with those with whom we are angry, petition against something we feel is wrong, campaign, or write a letter of complaint. Whatever we do, we must do something constructive with that anger.

Bitterness eats into us and is usually as a result of something that happened in the past. The chances are that we cannot change it so we must move on. It's in the past. We must leave it in the past and learn from it. Whoever has generated that feeling inside us will one day have to pay for it; we must not pay for it ourselves by ruining our health over it.

Revenge is not sweet, however much we may think it is. By wreaking revenge we create more pain and animosity, and this can be part of a vicious circle that comes back to hit us once again. We must avoid it by moving on. We should have learned a valuable lesson by what we suffered. We should now know how to avoid it happening again, and ensure that we never inflict such harm on another.

In the same way, vindictiveness and spitefulness is so non-productive. Why don't we turn a frown into a smile, a barb into a kind word? We would be pleasantly surprised how good that can feel, and there will be no adrenalin racing around with nowhere to go but to bring us down.

And of course there is hatred. What provokes such a strong and destructive emotion?

Hatred can be a product of hurt, fear, ignorance and misunderstanding. Hatred of a person who has hurt us in some way is non-productive too, and does our health no good at all. We must try to put it aside until such time, should the opportunity occur, we can ask the person in a reasonable way why they acted as they did. Aggression provokes aggression; that is not the way to go. If such a course of action is not feasible then we must feel sorry for the perpetrators who will have to ask for our forgiveness one day, and carry the burden of what they have done. Once we can summon up a little compassion, then that red will disappear and we will feel so much better.

Sadly, hatred comes in many forms and we are only too aware of the intense feeling behind racial hatred. But racial hatred is often also as a result of fear, ignorance or misunderstanding, and by learning more about that which has brought about our strong feelings, we may find those feelings dissipate. Understanding people, their feelings, their motives, their customs and *their* fears can change our own feelings and bring tolerance and compassion into our aura.

However hard we try to rid ourselves of the red in us, it will always appear from time to time because we are human, but as long as we understand it and work towards making its stay only temporary, it will not harm us.

PINK

When we have mastered the red in us, then we will find the pink. This is because pink represents the balance of our emotions. The best kind of unselfish love, kindness, compassion, tolerance, and understanding are represented in that pink aura. Not easily attained, but once gained we and others will benefit from our levelheaded approach to life. We will have learned that taking on other people's problems is not the way to go, and however much we care for and help them, we are able to step back and not carry the burden ourselves. It can take a while to achieve but what an achievement!

WHITE

We associate white with purity, and perhaps we can do so here too, for white represents a balance of our thoughts, not allowing them to be influenced by selfishness, materialism, negativity or anything else not conducive to a spiritual thought or feeling.

White is a supplement to other thoughts and feelings and will accompany other colours in the aura. To be able to balance our thoughts should be the ultimate aim with us all. The quality of life and how we live it, how we view life and how we view others will completely change once we have acquired this balance.

BLUE

Blue shows spirituality. Once we are back in the Spirit World, when we see blue in an aura we will know that it is reflecting great spirituality!

However, on the Earth Plane, Spirit uses this colour purely as a symbol of depression. Should we see blue with a person, we are being given a symbolic message by Spirit to tell us that this person is low in spirits, and the darker the blue the more depressed they are. Blue has often been seen as an indication that a person is receiving healing. What is really being shown is that this person is in *need* of healing and subsequently is feeling down.

PURPLE

Purple is the rich colour that in the material world is associated with royalty.   Purple in an aura indicates another kind of richness; that of a person who is embracing all spiritual thinking and feeling.   Wealth indeed, but only momentary, as we are living in a material world and we have to deal with material matters. Human thoughts and emotions will intrude, and the purple will fade from the aura to be replaced by other colours.

Purple can be seen when someone is in meditation and is indicative of the great spirituality of those who are working with them from the Spirit World.

There are several colours that have not been included in the aura colours and yet are often seen with one person or another. What does that mean?
The other colours you mention would be given by Spirit to tell you something about that person - they are purely symbolic:

a grass green would indicate the naturalness of that person, somebody who is true to themselves and does not pretend to be something they are not. A turquoise would indicate the 'new' age, the age of Aquarius; gold would indicate the spirituality of the wisdom being imparted at the time.

Is it possible to have your aura 'straightened'?

Remembering that the aura is but a reflection of *your* thoughts and *your* feelings, nobody but you can alter it in any way. However, should you be feeling low and somebody tells you that they can straighten your aura, then if you *believe* they can do so, the so called straightening *will* make you feel better and thus your aura will reflect a positivity that formerly you did not have. This is a case of autosuggestion, much as in the case of doctors giving placebos to patients. If the patients believe the tablets will help them, then there is a strong possibility that they will.

You must remember that only you can change your aura by your way of thinking and feeling. You are in control and nobody else!

Why is there such a difference of opinion with regard to the meanings of the aura colours?

This is because so many people interpret them in the way that they *feel* they should be interpreted, but they have not consulted Spirit. Each of these meanings has been given straight from our spirit teachers, who have been repeatedly questioned in order to be clear on every point, and they have made corrections when necessary.

People tend to confuse the aura colours with the colours of the rainbow, but the colours of the rainbow are connected to the physical world, whereas the aura colours are connected to your spirit.

It is difficult to change people's views on the meaning of the colours but Spirit can but try.

The Symbols

Every thought that comes into the mind becomes a picture. It is not possible to have a thought without that process taking place. Whatever the result that may ensue, the concept was in a picture, perhaps unnoticed, that appeared in your mind.

Working with symbols, we discover that every picture tells a story which is often more understandable than mere words would be. Symbols are a method of communication that has been around as long as mankind has occupied this planet. Whereas the easiest way to communicate on a one to one basis is of course speech, there has always been the need to convey information to those with whom you are not in personal touch and do not have a common written language - the need to leave a message, the need to tell a story. This is where symbols have such an important part to play

We associate symbols with the pictures found in caves or the hieroglyphics discovered in the pyramids but the use of symbols is not confined to the Stone Age or to Egypt, for we use symbols regularly in our everyday existence. The motorist interprets symbols whenever he takes his vehicle on the road, for what is each road sign if not a symbol? Even children when crossing the road use that same code of symbols.

How would those people who are unfortunate to have little or no hearing, manage without their sign language? It is a language in itself and consists of nothing but symbols. You will find symbols in shops and public buildings, showing the fire exits, the public conveniences, symbols on public transport, in the workplace and in every walk of life.

So why are we reluctant to learn the language of symbols? So much can be achieved with but a little effort from us. Most of what is communicated to us from the Spirit World has a much deeper meaning to it, so often missed because people take things at face value and look no further, even when the message makes no sense to them. The wisdom and guidance imparted from the Spirit World is lost to many people, because they do not know the language of the spirit symbols and do not realise that something so valuable can be acquired by a little understanding and a little work.

Mediums have so often passed on a message, unaware that they have failed to interpret the full meaning of the guidance, solely through ignorance of spirit symbols. Thus the true value and the essence of the communication are lost.

Knowledge of the language of symbols would be of such benefit to those who endeavour to understand the dreams that they have had. For it is through those dreams that stay with us and refuse to be forgotten that those in the spirit world send guidance, so often in vain. With a little knowledge of this language, the help, reassurance, comfort and warnings regularly conveyed to us via our dreams, would be at our fingertips.

When communicating with our spirit helpers, they will often use a symbol to illustrate a point, or to confine their message to the recipient and not to any other in the vicinity. It is therefore important that these symbols are interpreted correctly. The following list is an aid to understanding. It is not possible to include every symbol that may be used, but once having understood many of the basic meanings you should be able in time, to translate others yourself. Sometimes a symbol will have more than one meaning – often very different – you will learn to know within yourself which is the correct interpretation.

There are several basic symbols which are outlined first:

Water Water is symbolic of life. We cannot survive without it. It features symbolically so often in our every day lives. We talk about keeping our heads above water; we can feel as if we are swimming against the tide; we can feel lost, all at sea; we may be looking for a safe harbour; we can pour oil on troubled waters – the list goes on.

The sea of life, in which we are all swimming, can be as calm as a millpond, but it can also be stormy and the waves can knock us off our feet. We may feel that things are getting on top of us and that we are going to drown. We may even reach rock bottom and then sometimes we have to weigh anchor and move on.

Then of course we can be in the river of life where things are going along quite smoothly, but even there you can have a few ripples, which can touch other people's lives.

Fish Just as we are swimming along in the sea of life, so we can be likened to fish. We are all symbolically one kind of fish or another.

You could, for instance, be a goldfish, swimming around and around in a circle and not getting anywhere. Perhaps you are a salmon, someone who is a survivor, who has to swim against the stream, but whose way of life is based on control.

You will meet many different fish during your life. You may come across a shark and have to move away from it. Alternatively you may know a dolphin, who works in harmony with you, balancing its feelings so that they are never dangerously out of control.

Have you ever felt like a tiddler in a pond? It could be a pond polluted by other people's thoughts and actions, and you may have had to feel your way cautiously, as your vision has been impaired by that which is around you.

Boats We can be symbolised as boats too – boats on the sea of life, and we all have to paddle our own canoe, get on with our lives and not rely on others.

A steamboat is someone who has a lot of power and gets through life under their own steam, not rushing, going at a steady pace.

A sailing boat or yacht shows someone who has a balanced way of looking at, and coping with life. But they must ensure they do not allow someone else to take the helm i.e. take control of their life.

You may be a passenger boat, a liner perhaps, who carries many people in life. Or you could be a lifeboat helping those who feel they are drowning in a stormy period of their lives.

Animals We are all animals. Life is a jungle. We are animals in that jungle. A gazelle is very quick to detect danger.
Perhaps you are a mother hen, or know one. She looks after her brood, she wants everyone to be safe and sound and tries to take the world under her wing. You have to be careful with tigers. They claw and leave their mark; they creep up on you and pounce. Pythons twist around you and squeeze, they put their venom into you, poison your mind. You are left feeling emotionally and physically drained. But smaller snakes are representative of healing relating to the medical emblem of two snakes coiled around a staff. Birds - we are all birds. A peacock is proud to show its true colours and likes to be heard. A dove is a person who brings peace; someone who is a peacemaker.

Buildings Again we can all be symbolically represented by a building. A person represented as a cinema is someone who is always willing to entertain people, is never at a loss for words, and will open the door to allow people in and have the opportunity to rest and relax. Alternatively, a castle is a person who has erected his own fortress against others intruding in his life. This measure has been taken because of his experiences in life. If you are represented as a flat, this is showing exactly how you are feeling – flat and isolated, whereas if you were shown as a detached house, this would indicate that you detach yourself from others, are a loner.

Garden A garden represents your life and what you have put into it. A garden that is untidy and overgrown shows that you have some work to do in putting your life in order. An empty garden reflects just how little you have put into your life. A pathway in your garden that twists and turns shows that that is how your life has been, twisting and turning. A crazy paving shows that the twists and turns have really been crazy – quite unexpected. A garden that is in order shows that your life is in order.

Flowers   In the same way that fish represent people in the sea of life, so flowers are also representative of people in their garden of life. We are all flowers. Perhaps you are a daisy, the sort of person who, however many times cut down in life, springs back up again. A poppy symbolises someone or something to be remembered or someone who has been reminiscing. A daffodil is either someone who speaks out positively or someone who *needs* to use the trumpet and speak out in a positive way – perhaps assert themselves more. An orchid is a person who is rare, and needs careful nurturing. If this is you, do not sell yourself too cheaply. Recognise your value. Roses are all to do with love because roses have a heart. A red rose is someone giving pure love from the world of Spirit, a white rose is a thank you, and yellow is a message about your positive attitude.

Fruit and Vegetables   Fruit and vegetables all represent people.A pear is always representative of a man – the rough skin – and the tomato of a woman – softness. A banana shows somebody who needs a little straightening out but who is positive about himself and life in general and who, deep inside, is one of the best, the cream. An apple is telling you that you have the ability to pass on wisdom to others, a teacher but not necessarily one from the classroom, a teacher about life. An orange represents wisdom, someone who has learned from life and who has plenty within to share with others but whether it is used for the benefit of others or themselves is very much up to them. It may well be used for devious means. A gooseberry is someone who can be rather thick-skinned – insensitive not recognising when his presence is unwanted. A strawberry indicates someone who is easily squashed emotionally. A pineapple is a person who is rather prickly to handle and has a tough skin. A person who is represented by a grape is one who has it within him to enrich his life. It shows a different way of living, taking away the blandness of the life previously led. The cucumber shows negativity with little substance. A person represented as a lettuce is someone who needs to be with others, is no good alone, but who mixes well.

Trees Trees always have a family connection – the family tree, your roots. A branch is part of the family and a twig is the younger member of that family. A wooden spoon indicates that somebody is 'stirring' in the family.

Hats These show something that is on ahead (on a head), something in the future, and the kind of hat you have will give you further information. A headscarf shows that everything will be tied up and in place, secure. A skullcap reflects something that is close ahead. If there is a feather in it, it would mean a feather in your cap, signifying something you would have achieved. A bonnet with fruit on shows that you will receive the fruits of your labour. A Tyrolean hat, worn by a yodeller, shows that there will be something ahead for which you will need to use your voice.

Vehicles Once more, these are representative of people, the physical body carrying the spirit within. A coach is a person who coaches or teaches. An ambulance is someone who heals, not necessarily a healer of the physical body. A Rolls Royce represents somebody who is the best of his kind.

Food You many describe someone as being 'as soft as butter,' and anyone would understand that you are referring to a person so kind and compassionate that they can be taken advantage of. Milk quite naturally represents mother. Father is represented by something from the same source but a little harder – cheese. Cream is for a grandmother figure, someone who has had time to mature into something especially good. Bread represents spiritual words – manna from Heaven; it feeds the spirit. Honey also feeds within, and is of great value spiritually. Beef would indicate a 'beefcake', a man who is all muscle, full of himself, self-important, whereas a cheesecake is a father figure whose life is based on a good material foundation.

A

Abscess A verbal problem that must be 'opened up' – acknowledged, discussed, in order to get rid of poisonous feelings held within.

Academy A person who has attained great wisdom through the academy (their experiences) of life.

Accordion Someone who has it in their own hands to avoid being emotionally squeezed.

Ace Someone who is 'one of the best'.

Acorn The onset of the ability to grow and become strong within.

Acrobat A need to get a greater grip on yourself or a situation.

Actor/actress Someone able to mask their feelings, put on a face for the occasion and be many people.Someone who will *need* to mask their feelings.

Advertisement Someone will be announcing news in the hope that you will be able to see (understand) something.

Aerial Signifies a need to communicate.

Aeroplane A person who is ready to take off and able to take an overall view of life.

Aftershave The finishing touch after all has been sorted out – things 'smell' nicer now.

Agent Someone who works for others.

Alarm Take heed of a warning.

Albatross A person who is very aware of the dangers in life.

Alien Someone who is different. There is a situation with which you are not comfortable.

Alps Someone who has had to climb many mountains in life and even then, having reached the summit, has still to take care, watch his step (snow – hazard).

Alleyway A warning that taking short cuts can be dangerous.

Alsatian A male who is strong and protective and can represent law and order.

Ambulance A person who gives healing to others. A situation that needs to be dealt with quickly – an emergency.

Animals All kinds of people. We are animals in the jungle of life – the kind of animal is important.

Anchor A person who is prevented from moving on in life by a situation that keeps them in the same place. There is a need to 'weigh anchor' and move on. The need to drop anchor, stay for a while and take stock.

Angel A messenger bringing spiritual help and guidance.

Antelope A person who can hurt with direct confrontation.

Antique Someone of great value from the past. Someone who needs to be valued.

Ants People who are industrious and are team workers. They are loyal to their own and have the strength of character to carry others on their back in times of trouble.

Ape Someone who copies what others do; hasn't got a mind of their own.

Apostle A person who is very spiritual and is always in service to others.

Apple A teacher – sharing the fruits of their wisdom. Able to communicate with others. Red apple – a teacher who gets too emotionally involved. Toffee apple – something in life to be licked and chewed over before you are able to teach others from it.

Apple pie A person who teaches about life, teachings that can be shared and enjoyed by many. They try to teach to the highest standard – in apple pie order.

Apron Preparation for dirty work to be sorted out.

Apron (maid's) Ready and willing to serve others.

Aquarium A situation in which your freedom is limited and you have no place to hide.

Armour A protection that does not allow others to get through (to hurt).

Ark A person who gives shelter or refuge.

Arrow A situation in which you will be shown the way to go.

Ashes An emotional situation that has now burned out. The aftermath of an emotional situation.

Asleep Be more awake to what is going on around you – open your eyes!

Ass Someone who makes a fool of themselves.

Assault A person or a situation that is 'getting at you'.

Asylum Seeking a place of safety from life's traumas.

Athlete Someone who works hard to achieve.

Atlas Somebody who takes the world on their shoulders – (other people's problems)

Attic The mind.

Aubergine A person who will try their best to think and feel with the highest motives but who needs at times to have their feet on the ground.

Aura A situation from which you will be able to see the light - a positive outcome.

Aviary People who have limited freedom.

Avocado Somebody who is very negative with not much of a personality (bland).

Axis Keeping the balance.

B

Baby A new beginning or happening.

Baby's safety pin Safety – make it a point to be careful in connection with a new beginning.

Back Something that is now behind you; get on with your life.

Bacon Saving someone in a difficult situation, in trouble – saving someone's bacon.

Badge Something that has been earned and which announces who and what you are.

Badger Someone who pesters.

Bag Luggage (experiences from life) that you take around with you. A carrier – a person carrying other people's personal problems.

Bagpipes A person who is full of wind - has a lot to say of little consequence.

Balcony A person able to extend themselves, which enables them to improve their outlook and to get things out in the open.

Bald There seems to be nothing on ahead for this person.

Ball Someone who can bounce back – the colour of the ball is significant – check with the aura colours. Someone who is up and down. Tennis ball – a situation between two people.

Ballerina A person who is always on their toes. There is a need to be on your toes. Someone who is well balanced.

Ballet shoes Keeping on your toes. Red ballet shoes – keep on your toes where emotional situations are concerned.

Balloon A need or ability to rise above a situation or problem (the colour is significant). A celebration.

Banana You have a positive outlook but need to open up a situation in order to sort it out. There is need to straighten yourself out in a positive way to find the best, the cream within.

Band A group of people who can harmonise, get on well together.

Bandage An emotional wound that needs tending (sorting out and wrapping up).

Banjo Someone who brings happiness and upliftment to others.

Bank Powerhouse, providing power (currency) to be used for the good of others. Is strong and dependable.

Banner Letting something be known. If the banner has 'Finish' displayed on it, it means it is the end of a situation.

Bar Serves Spirit.

Bare A situation that has been exposed, uncovered.

Bark A male whose bark is worse than his bite.

Barrel A fun person, larger than life.

Bar steward Someone who is in service to help others.

Barbie doll A person who has nothing going for them – no personality.

Base A situation or experience upon which you are now able to build A strong foundation that will be a good support in the future.

Basket A woven basket – someone is blind about a situation. Someone is prevaricating - in and out around the issue without making a decision or commitment.

Basket of fruit Each piece of fruit is a symbol in itself to be interpreted.

Bat Blind to a situation.

Bath Preparation. Clearing the way for a future task.

Bathing hat Something close on ahead to do with other people (in a pool, meaning with other people). Orange bathing hat – as above, but with the need to deal with it wisely.

Bathroom Place of preparation for a situation that needs sorting out.

Battery Somebody who has only a limited power and a time limit within which to use it.

Battlefield A problem or situation which left many people hurt in one way or another.

Beach Sands of time.

Beach ball A person who gets through life by being a colourful, bouncy person.

Beacon Somebody who is a light for others; is there to guide the way in the storms of life.

Beak An insignificant verbal attack (peck).

Beans Someone full of beans and is going to have more fun in life. A need to have more fun in life. Tin of beans with lid on – feelings are controlled (contained) within but are pent up inside and should be released. Broad bean – a person willing to broaden their outlook, and who works well with others. Runner bean – a social climber.

Bear A person of great strength and comfort.

Beard Someone who won't face up to things.

Beaver A person who works continuously trying to help themselves and others – will not give in.

Bed Life. The state of the bed is important e.g. an unmade bed indicates that the state of the person's life is untidy, disorganised and needs to be tidied up. Four poster bed – the person has a lot of support in their life.

Bed bug A person in your life who is draining and annoying you.

Bedcover The image you present to others in life. Candlewick bedspread – showing that your life is not smooth and has lots of highs and lows.

Bedroom What is going on in life around you.

Beetroot Somebody who does not have control of their emotions and who loses their temper very quickly.

Beggar Someone who takes from others.

Belt Someone who is able to give support and prevent things falling apart.

Bench (garden) A situation that is out in the open, concerning more than one person. Someone who is being judged by another.

Beret Something ahead that can flatten you. Red beret – something that can flatten you emotionally.

Berry A small insignificant person.

Betting office Someone who likes to take a gamble, hedges their bets.

Bike Well balanced and pushing ahead with your own efforts.

Binoculars Seeing things more clearly and in greater detail.

Bird A person – the type of bird is indicative of the person's character.

Birdcage Someone who is feeling 'caged', no freedom to do as they wish, trapped in a situation. Birdcage with door open – freedom.

Bird's nest Someone who has worked hard to provide for their young.

Biscuit Someone with a lot of cheek.

Black and white Plain to see. A person who likes things in black and white – no in-between but who needs to bring a little colour into their life.

Blackbird A very spiritual person whose words are also spiritual.

Blackboard A lesson in life from which you should learn. A blackboard with blue and white chalks – a lesson in balancing the depressing (blue) side of yourself by thinking in a different way.

Blanket A situation in life where the truth is hidden. A need for comfort.

Bleach A person who needs to balance their way of thinking (bleach whitens).

Blind A situation in which you are not seeing something.

Blister A situation that has rubbed you up the wrong way.

Block of offices Person who is surrounded by many on different levels; far seeing if given the chance but can also be hemmed in by those around them.

Blonde Someone who is going to be enlightened (on ahead).

Blood Seeing red (angry)

Blossom A person who is about to blossom out, will now do well.

Blue Feeling down, depressed, feeling blue.

Bluebell A person who has the 'blues', needing a listening ear. Somebody who holds a lot of wisdom because of life's experiences.

Bollard There to keep you on the right side of life.

Bomb A situation that is going to explode.

Bonsai (tree) Someone who has deliberately been kept down in life.

Book A person A dark green book – a negative person (see aura colours). A yellow book –a positive person.

Bookcase Someone who holds a lot of wisdom.

Bottle A person. Someone who is bottling things up and should release the pent up emotion inside. A dark green bottle – a person who is feeling very negative about life or a situation. A bottle of bleach – a person who can help others to balance their way of thinking.

Bottom A situation you are sitting on. It's now time to move on.

Bouquet A bunch of people, different flowers – different people.

Box A situation where you feel boxed in (confined).

Boxer A person who is a fighter in life.

Boxing gloves A fight in life that is in your own hands to sort out.

Bra Upliftment, support for you in the future.

Bracelet Something around you, something already there on hand.

Brake A need to slow down.

Brass Top brass – the best.

Bread Spiritual food - will sustain you in life. Mouldy bread – spiritual wisdom that is not being used.

Breakfast (full English) Someone who starts off with a lot on his plate.

Brew To bring about good or bad. Something is brewing.

Brick A decent person. A hod of bricks – take care. Do not overload yourself; you could be carrying too many people

Bridge A link, a contact. A cast iron bridge – the strength to overcome a problem.

Briefcase A person who comes straight to the point (brief).

Bright light Things are going to brighten up for you.

Broccoli A negative person.

Brooch In connection with a material situation, it is keeping things in place in an attractive (acceptable) way.

Broom A person who helps to sweep away the rubbish in life.

Bucket A person always ready to help and clean up for others in life.

Budgerigar Someone who brings brightness into people's lives and gives more than someone of a greater stature or better means. A giver – able to live on a small budget. A generous, happy (chirpy) person.

Buffalo A man who has the strength to cope with life.

Bug Someone who lives off others.

Bull Somebody who charges into situations without thinking.

Bull dog A man who has great determination and strength.

Bungalow Someone who is on the level – what you see is what you get.

Burial A situation that is going to be buried – finished with.

Burning bush A person who is emotionally fiery. A person who has a high temperature.

Bursar Somebody who disposes power (currency) to others.

Bus A person who carries a lot of people in life; a person who takes other people's problems on board.

Busy bee A person who is always busy.

Butcher's A meeting place.

Buttercup A very positive person who makes their point in their own way, even if it goes unnoticed.

Butterfly A release from a situation. Someone who is emerging from a period of inactivity and is now ready to take off. Someone willing to change for the better.

Buzzard A person who is mean - would pick you dry.

C

Cabbage A person who is being negative about something, who needs to be motivated (or else they will vegetate).

Cage A person who feels imprisoned.

Cake A sweeter communication.

Call There is someone trying to attract your attention.

Camel A person who has 'got the hump' about something.

Camera A person who is inclined to snap and tends to remember things from the past (negative or positive).

Camouflage A situation linked to a person who is covering up something – be aware.

Camp fire Something out in the open that is linked with emotions.

Camphor balls (moth balls) A protection against a material problem.

Candle There will be a light to brighten the darkness of a situation.

Canoe A person who manages to paddle their way through life on their own.

Car A person - the physical body. Open-topped car – someone who likes to be noticed; a person who is too open (vulnerable).

Caravan Someone who has no roots; is always on the move.

Cardigan A person who gives an extra touch of warmth to someone in need.

Carousel A situation where you are going round and round and not getting anywhere but you have the means to stop it and get off.

Carpet Something that is underfoot – a current situation (colour is important)

Carrot An enticer, something to encourage you to go forward, to keep your interest.

Castle Someone who is a loner and who protects themselves from outside influences; it is difficult to penetrate their shell.

Cat Woman.

Caterpillar A situation from which you are going to be set free. You have been contained for long enough.

Cathedral Someone who can be a little awe inspiring. He aspires to greater things and is at home with the beauty of the soul.

Cauliflower Someone who needs to have his ears boxed because he will not listen (cauliflower ear).

Celery A person who is straight with you – no nonsense. Can be crisp and concise when dealing with other people.

Cellar The lower self, the darker or negative side of a person.

Cello A person who has both feet firmly on the ground when speaking on issues that give pleasure.

Cement There is a situation where there is a need to bond together with another person – cement a friendship.

Chains Linked with many people. A person who has many friends. A situation that restricts freedom.

Chair A situation you are sitting on. A chair with a worn blue seat – an old situation that has kept you down for years.

Champagne Celebration.

Chandelier A group of enlightened people who give out a lot of love.

Cheese Father or father figure. Cottage cheese – father who is too soft.

Cheesecake Someone who is a father figure who provides a good material (brown) base upon which to build.

Cheetah A female who cheats.

Cheque There is a situation where something needs to be checked.

Cherry Nothing i.e. 'Life is just a bowl of cherries' means a bowl of nothing – nothing to it, nothing to get het up about.

Cherub A person who is loving and well loved – precious.

Chest There is something in front (ahead of you) that will need to be sorted, to be got rid of (get it off your chest).

Chewing gum Someone who likes to chew over things. Something to chew over before taking action.

Chicken A person who is a 'mother hen' who looks after her brood; she wants everyone to be safe and sound; she tries to get the world under her wing.

Child A person who is acting childishly and has a lot to learn in life.

Children A group of people who are acting childishly.

Chimney A release from an emotional situation.

Chips Someone who will be given their marching orders.

Chocolate bar Something to do with the material life that needs to be shared equally with others. A box of chocolates – a lot of people, each with a different centre (character), and each with a different problem.

Choke There is a situation with someone who has a verbal problem. Be careful.

Church A person who has built up a great fund of spiritual knowledge – the spiritual you within (inner temple).

Cigar A warning about something in your material life.

Cigarette A health warning.

Cinema A person who is always willing to entertain people, will open their doors to many people, giving them the opportunity to settle down and relax.

Clap A situation where you are going to be pleased with yourself or others will be pleased with you.

Clarinet A person who has control of the words they speak at their fingertips.

Cliff edge Watch your step!

Cloak To cloak the real identity to disguise feelings or allegiances.

Clock A person. Type of clock important e.g. Grandfather clock. Someone who takes life at a steady pace. Something is being noted (clocked).

Clothes A link with a material matter.

Clothes line A material problem needs to be brought out into the open.

Clouds Problems that are overshadowing you.

Clover Things are now going well.

Clown A person who appears bright and cheerful on the surface, but who is sad underneath; a person who masks their feelings. A clown with a red face – as above, but embarrassed by their actions.

Club A meeting place of people with like minds.

Coach (vehicle) To help, teach or coach.

Coal A wealth of learning gleaned from being 'in the pits' – the darkness of despair.

Coat Physical body.

Coconut A person who is hard to crack, but once you get through you will find the best within.

Coconut shy A hard 'nut' who avoids dealing with a situation.

Coffee Be alert to what is going on.

Coffin An ending to a situation; putting something to rest.

Coil A need to unwind. Are you allowing someone to wind you up?

Coins Currency – spiritual power.

Cold There is an unfriendly feeling around you.

Collage A life that has been put together with many and varied experiences.

College A person who has learned much through their experiences in life and is in a position to teach others.

Comb Sorting out things ahead; untangling a situation. The colour of the comb is significant. A brown comb is to do with a material problem, a yellow comb is something positive.

Commando Someone who will tackle life's situations, regardless of the odds.

Computer The brain.

Container A vase, suitcase, tin etc. All are containers and are symbolic of people (containers of the spirit).

Cork A person who bobs along in life, will not let life's problems pull them under.

Corn (wheat) Something that has grown from a seed planted in the mind.

Corn (on the foot) An annoying situation caused by pressure and affecting your direction in life.

Corset Someone who needs to shape up to things. Something that will bring you into line.

Cottage Someone who is comfortable to be with.

Cotton wool There is a need for you to look after yourself more.

Countryside Something that is out in the open.

Cow Mother or mother figure.

Corned beef A male who is difficult to get through to until you have the key to their character.

Crab A person who is irritable (crabby).

Cracker Someone who is being pulled in two directions and who is waiting for the explosion!

Cradle A safe haven for a new beginning.

Cream Grandmother or grandmother figure.

Cross A burden you carry in life.

Crossword A puzzle in life to be solved.

Crow Someone who keeps on and on. Someone who 'crows' about something.

Crown The best is ahead.

Cruiser A person able to cruise through life. Will only take on board those who are like-minded (fighter).

Crush Emotions are at breaking point.

Cry There is a need for help. A release from an emotional problem.

Crystal Someone valuable. Seeing something clearly.

Cub A male who has not had much experience of life; a need to grow up.

Cuckoo A person who makes a lot of fuss and noise about things and is known to exploit other people.

Cuckoo clock The time is right to stop a person or people imposing on you.

Cucumber Negative, a person with no substance within.

Cup Vessel, a person. Someone who is on their own and needs support (the saucer).

Cup of tea A need to take a break.

Curtains Outlook on life.Crushed velvet curtains – someone whose outlook has been crushed by life's experiences.Net curtains – able to see what is going on outside without people intruding on your privacy.

Custard Something that makes a situation more palatable.

D

Daffodil Someone who speaks out, or needs to speak out in a positive way, with conviction. Needs to blow their trumpet more.

Dagger A warning to be aware that someone could be doing some 'back stabbing'.

Daisy Someone who, no matter how many times cut down in life, springs back up again.

Dalmatian A man who is 'spot on' when sizing people up.

Damson A kind woman who at times can be taken advantage of.

Dancing Someone who is not behaving themselves – leading you a merry dance.A situation where there is a need to keep in step with another in order to sort it out.

Dandelion A person with an iron will, used in a positive way.

Darkness A situation in which you have been 'kept in the dark'.Someone who has lost their way. Someone going through a feeling of doom and gloom, and who needs brightening.

Darning needle A situation where you have to 'make do and mend'.

Dart A person who gets to the point quickly.A situation where it is necessary for the goal to be reached without delay.

Dart board The goal to aim for.

Dawn It is time for you to wake up to a situation around you – recognise what is going on.

Decay An ongoing situation now nearing its end.

Decorate There is a need for you to change your outlook.

Decorator Someone who helps to brighten your outlook.

Deaf A situation in which you are 'turning a deaf ear.' There is a need for you to listen.

Death Ending of a situation.

Dent A situation in which your pride has been hurt.

Desert Deserted, barren – nothing going on in life at the moment.

Detached house A person who is a loner, likes to be alone to do their 'own thing'.

Diamond A person of great worth.Rough diamond – someone who needs to be shaped and polished.

Diary You, the person, must not allow anyone else to dictate or interfere with your plans or schedule.

Dice A person who is always prepared to take a chance in life.

Dictionary A person who has the ability to understand words of wisdom.

Dig A need to delve more into something that is happening at the moment (underfoot).A person who is getting to you verbally (having a dig).

Dinghy A small- minded person whose ego is easily inflated.

Diploma Someone who has passed many tests with honour in the University of Life.

Directory A person with many contacts in life, and who is straight when dealing with others.

Dirt A situation underfoot needs cleaning up.

Disinfectant A person who cleans up after people's misfortunes.

Dispensary A person who is able to dispense healing advice (to make one feel better within).

Disguise A person who is not what they seem.

Diver A person who is able to plumb the depths of life and still be able to rise to the surface.

Divorce The cutting off from a situation.

Dock A situation where you are now able to rest after an experience (the sea of life).

Doctor A healer of emotional problems.

Dog Adult male

Doll Female: China doll – a female who is fragile. Rag doll – a female with no backbone.someone who is weary.

Doll's house A person who is only playing at life, and who needs to grow up and face responsibility.

Dolphin A good, kind, loving and altogether nice person.

Donkey Someone who is used too much by others – 'flogged'.

Door Mouth – to do with speaking, what is said etc.An opening (opportunity) is going to be presented to you.

Door mat Someone who is being taken advantage of.

Dormouse A timid person who is taken advantage of by others.

Dove Peace

Drain A situation that is draining you – you need revitalising.

Drake A man who is able to stay on top of things in life.

Dress Something that needs to be addressed – the colour of the dress is significant.

Dressing gown A need to rest more – relax.

Drill (tool) A person who can be a bore.

Drill (march) Someone who needs to keep in step with life.

Drowning Someone who is out of their depth in a situation – take care.

Drowsy Someone who needs to wake up and become more alive to what is going on around them.

Drum Getting the message across, broadcasting, making yourself heard. Beating the drum – communication.

Duck Person who glides through life easily. If it has a yellow beak, they have a very positive attitude to life. Always able to ride the storms in life, stays on top of things.

Dummy Someone who comforts with words. Someone who needs comforting.

Dungarees A worker.

Dungeon A person who has a negative attitude to life and who is imprisoned within themselves.

Dustbin A person with a lot of rubbish in their life that they must get rid of.

E

Eagle A person able to rise above things and see things more clearly.

Earring Within a year. Two earrings – within 2 years.

Earth A person who is down to earth.

Eel Someone who is slippery – not easy to hold down.

Egg A new beginning. Something that is going to hatch out. Hard boiled egg – someone hard boiled. Hard boiled egg – a new beginning that is going stale. Act on it before it is too late.

Elastic A person or situation being stretched too far. A person who can snap.

Elbow A person or situation that needs to be put out of your life (given the elbow).

Elder flower An older person whose view on life is balanced and refreshing.

Elephant A situation linked with an older, female member of the family who needs to be listened to.

Embryo The start of a new beginning.

Emu A person who gets on with life but is not a high flyer.

Encyclopaedia A knowledgeable person.

Engagement ring A commitment to a circle of people.

Engine The heart. Steam engine – someone able to get along under their own steam and is able to help others along.

Engineer Someone who arranges (fixes) things for people.

Entertainer A person with a happy disposition.

Envelope A person carrying news.

Eskimo A person able to cope with the emotionally cold conditions of life.

Ewe A female who follows others (sheep).

Exam A situation that is testing your abilities.

Executioner A person who has the ability to put an end to situations.

Exercise bike (and exercise treadmill) need to exercise the mind, get on the treadmill of life and expand your thinking. A need to physically exercise more.

Explorer A person who is ready or needs to seek another way out of the situation.

Explosion A situation ready to blow up in your face!

Extinguisher Someone who is able to dampen down or put out a fiery situation.

Eye Someone who is not seeing things, should open their eyes to what is happening in their life. A situation where you should keep an eye on things.

F

Face Something ahead that you have to face.

Factory A very busy person who rarely rests, always on the go, doesn't keep enough time for themselves.

Fairy A person who steps lightly, conscious of not hurting others' feelings.

Falcon A person who will attack others less able to defend themselves.

Fall You are heading for a fall – be careful.

Falling A feeling of not being in control, connected with something that is going on in your life.

Fan There will be a situation in which you will need to 'keep cool'.

Fanfare The welcome result of something for which you have been waiting.

Fang A person who has the ability to hurt others with biting comments.

Fan mail A need to 'keep cool' in a situation linked with a communication.

Farm A collection of different types of people (animals).

Farmer A person who sows seeds of wisdom wherever they go.

Fatigue Rest and stand back from a situation that has been draining you.

Feather Feather in your cap – a commendation for something you have done or achieved. A purple feather in your cap – recognition for the contribution you have made for something very worthy.

Feet Direction in life. Whatever is covering your feet is symbolic of your direction. Wellington boots – you are protected in all conditions. Ballet shoes – you need to be on your toes. Workman's shoes – there is work for you to do. Workman's shoes with steel toecaps - all directions covered, nobody can step on your toes. Feet in mud – a muddy situation, be careful. Left foot – spiritual pathway or direction. Right foot – material pathway or direction.

Fence A feeling of being fenced in.

Fern A person able to adapt to any conditions.

Ferry A person always ready to help others through difficult periods of their lives..

Fertiliser Something to help your spiritual growth. Something to increase the quality of your life

Fete (fate) A situation that comes into your life that was meant to be, and could not be avoided.

Fiddle A person not to be trusted. In a material situation, a person who would 'fiddle'.

Field Pastures green – a new enterprise.

File A situation that needs to be kept in order.

Film Someone living in a fantasy world who needs to get their feet on the ground.

Finger Someone always on hand and is close to others.

Fire Emotions. Fire in the grate – love in the heart. An empty grate – nothing going for that person. No love there. Camp fire – making trouble concerned with people outside.

Fire engine Someone who rescues people from an emotional situation.

Fireguard The means to keep emotions under control - guarded.

148

Fireman Able to dampen down an emotional situation.

Fireplace The focal point of the emotions. Wooden fireplace – an emotional connection to the family. Marble fireplace – emotions are very cold.

Fish A person. A shark – a person not to be trusted. Plaice – a person who is feeling flat. Rainbow trout – a colourful person. Battered fish – someone who has taken a battering in life.

Fishing rod A situation where someone gets 'hooked'.

Fishmonger A 'fishy' person i.e. dubious character.

Flamingo A person who is emotionally well balanced.

Flannel (face) A person who can 'sweet talk' you and give you a load of waffle (nonsense).

Flask A person who contains their emotions – keeps them to themselves and doesn't allow them to change whether they are hot or cold.

Flat (apartment) Someone fed up, negative, depressed, flat, needing to build on what they have in order to find something worthwhile in life.

Flat feet Someone feeling flat who needs a lift to get started in the right direction.

Flea Someone who irritates others.

Fledgling A beginner.

Fleece Be wary of someone who takes from others (fleeces).

Fleet A collection of people able to work in harmony with one another on the sea of life.

Flood Uncontrollable emotions.

Floor What's underfoot – what is currently going on in your life.

Flower A person.

Flute Sweet music i.e. the words that are spoken are sweet – music to the ears. A brown flute – someone whose prospects in their material life is beginning to sound sweeter.

Fly Someone who is being 'fly' about something – knowing.

Foal The beginning of spiritual power.

Fog A situation in which you are unable to see where you are going (you are losing your direction in life).

Food Something to stimulate your thinking – food for thought. The type of food will indicate the lines in which the thinking should go e.g. a full English breakfast would suggest they have a lot on their plate from the start. Toast – heated words – linked with a material situation. Mushroom – a person who has grown from a dark period in their life.

Fool A person who does not take life seriously – fools around.

Foot Direction in life. The first step has been taken.

Football Someone who gets kicked about in life. Someone who has been kicked into touch.

Footprints A situation that has left its mark.

Forest The family

Fork A situation where words should be held back and not spoken – words are the food, and the fork secures the food.

Fort A person who is well protected - safe.

Fortune A wealth of wisdom.

Fossil A situation from the past that has been buried for a long time and has now been brought to light. A person still in the past, and who needs to move with the times.

Fox A person who is cunning.

Frame The physical body.

Freesia A person with sweetness of character.

Fried egg Keep your sunny side up.

Fringe (hair) A situation right in front of you that is going to be cut short.There is a need to cut it (the situation) short.

Frisbee A situation between two people that keeps going back and forth.

Frog A person whose mind is constantly on the move – hops from one thing to another. They must try to concentrate on one thing at a time.

Frown Someone is disapproving of something that is going to happen in the near future (in front).

Fruit People.Apple – teacher. Pineapple – a person who is thick-skinned and prickly.

Frying pan Someone whose emotions are laid bare, liable to overheat and could be a danger to themselves or others.

Fugitive A person running away from life.

Funeral The death of an event, a happening or situation put to rest.

Fungus A situation that has turned bad.

Fur Someone able to give out a lot of warmth.

Furnace Someone who is fiery within.

G

Gaffer Someone who can take control and whom others respect.

Gag A situation where things must remain unsaid.

Gale A situation that can be very stormy.

Galleon A person always there, ready to defend others' rights.

Gallery A colourful person with stories to tell.

Gambler A person who takes a chance in life.

Garage Somewhere to park yourself in safety to rest for a while.

Garden Your life and what you have put into it. An overgrown garden – your life needs sorting out. Garden of life – you reap what you sow.

Gardener A person who tries to help others to put their lives in order. Landscape gardener – a person who helps people to plan their lives.

Garden shears Something in your life needs to be trimmed back.

Gate Mouth – care should be taken in what is said outside the confines of your own home.

Gem A person of value.

General Someone who leads people through life's battles.

Gentry A person who feels he is above others.

Geranium A bright and constant personality.

Ghetto A situation from which it is difficult to escape.

Ghost Someone from the past.

Giant A person who is spiritually very large within.

Gift Something precious to be nurtured.

Giraffe Someone seeking to learn more about life, reaching upwards and who is far seeing.

Girder A person able to shoulder the weight (responsibility) of others.

Glacier A cold, frigid person.

Glade An opening (clearing) in a situation to do with the family.

Gladiator A person who is a fighter in life.

Gladiolus A person who is upright and straight with others.

Glass Somebody whom you can see through. A person who has nothing hidden.

Glasses There to help you to see things more clearly. A new pair of glasses – to see a situation differently. Reading glasses – to enable you to read into the situation.

Glove Something on hand to give you warmth and protection.

Glue A situation you are stuck with.

Glutton Someone who never learns from their mistakes – a glutton for punishment.

Gnome A male stuck in a rut in his life (garden).

Goat Grandfather or grandfather figure.

Gold The highest form of wisdom – the golden years. Gold ring – a good fund of wisdom is on hand.

Goldfish Someone trapped in a situation, going round and round and getting nowhere.

Golf ball A situation in which you may end up in a hole!

Gondola A romantic person.

Gong The time has come for you to be heard in an ongoing situation.

Gosling A person who has yet to grow, who is learning how to cope with life and how to glide through it.

Goose A silly person who does not think.

Governor Someone who likes to be in charge – in control.

Graduate A person who has learned a lot of the lessons of life and learned them well.

Grapes A situation where a better quality of life has been achieved.

Grass Something afoot that needs to be kept under control.

Grate The heart of the emotions. Empty grate – no love – nothing going for that person.

Grave A situation laid to rest.

Gravy A change for the better in a material situation.

Gravy boat A person who will bring a change for the better in a material situation.

Grease Take care – there is a situation where you could slip up.

Greenhouse A person who has a good all round view of life and who can nurture and give love to many. A person who is able to see all that is going on around them. A warm person with nothing hidden.

Grey The state of a current situation.

Grill A situation where questions need to be asked.

Guard A protector.

Guardian Someone who tries to keep you on the right pathway of life.

Guide book A person able to give a helping hand.

Guillotine Something in the future (ahead) that needs to be severed.

Gun Someone is gunning for you.

Gutter A situation that has made you feel at the lowest ebb in your life.

Gymnasium A person who is shaping up to things in life and sorting themselves out.

Gypsy A person who is restless and who likes to be on the move.

H

Haberdashery A person concerned with the little things in life that help to keep things together.

Hailstones A temporary situation where emotions are cold and hard.

Hair Something ahead.

Hairdresser Seeing to things ahead. Something being styled for the future, shaping up for the future, putting things in shape.

Hair band A group of people securing something for what is ahead.

Hair clip To secure something for ahead.

Haircut Something being cut back or restyled for the future. Short haircut – taking a short cut ahead. Hair tied back – something that is now behind you. There is no longer any need to be concerned about it. Curly hair – twists and turns on ahead. Straight hair – things are straight ahead.

Hairnet Keeping things in place for what is ahead.

Hall The passage of time.

Halo There is light ahead to get you through the darkness of this situation.

Hammer Something needs to be 'hammered home'; a point must be put across so that there is no misunderstanding.

Hammock Two in the family from whom you need to rest.

Hamster Someone always on the go.

Hand A person ready to help.

Handbag Something very personal that should be kept to yourself. A very personal situation.

Handcuffs A situation in which you are unable to help. Your 'hands are tied'.

Hand fork Something to help you to handle a situation in life (garden) without upsetting others.

Handkerchief Something in hand to help with an emotional situation – the colour is significant.

Handle There is something available to enable you to be in control – to handle it properly.

Harbour To provide you (the ship) with a place of safety.

Harlequin A colourful person who is good company.

Harness Allows you to be in control. Someone is controlling you.

Harp Someone who talks incessantly about something – 'harps on'. A person who is gentle and soothing in their communication with others.

Harpoon Someone who can hurt when making a point.

Harvest The result of what you sow in life. The time is ripe to reap what you have sown.

Hat All types of hats are symbolic of things ahead (on a head). Sun hat – protection from heated words. Cap – keeping something to yourself (keeping it under your hat/cap)

Hatch Bringing forward new thoughts to do with a new situation.

Hatchet A situation that should be buried.

Hawk A person who doesn't miss a thing.

Headlines Something that attracts your attention.

Headmaster A person who can help to make you aware of the lessons you are learning in life. Someone who has mastered things in life.

Hearse A person who can take something away to lay the situation to rest.

Heart An emotional situation.

Heaven A happy state of mind.

Hedge To be hedged in – confined, restricted. To keep a distance from others.

Heel Something that is behind you, enabling you to go forward in a new direction.

Helicopter Someone who needs to lift themselves. To rise above things quickly.

Hell A negative state of mind.

Helmet There to protect you against a dangerous situation ahead.

Hen A worrier, a 'mother hen' – someone who can be overprotective.

Herd A group of people of like minds.

Hermit A person who is a loner.

Highwayman A person who takes and does not give.

Hill A small problem, easy to overcome. Whatever is happening at the moment, stop making a mountain of it; it's not as big a problem as it seems!

Hippopotamus A person at home in muddy situations in life.

Hitchhiker A person who thinks life is a free ride.

Hive There is a lot going on – a hive of activity.

Hoe A situation in life which needs to be broken down into manageable pieces in order for the seeds of common sense to be sown.

Hog A greedy male.

Hole A situation from which you should step away before you get in any deeper.

Holly A negative and prickly person.

Honey A reward for hard work.

Hook Caught up in a situation.

Hoop There is a situation all around you, and you need to step out of it.

Hoover Someone who deals with other people's messes.

Hopscotch A need to keep on your toes, be agile and be careful where you tread. If you take your time and take care, you will arrive where you want to be.

Horn Horn of plenty – full of the good things in life.

Horse Power to be used for the good of mankind.

Hospital A person capable of giving healing and upliftment.

Hostel A person who gives of themselves to many people in need.

Hotel Someone who gives short-term help to people.

Hot water bottle Someone who gives warmth and comfort. Someone in need of comfort. A blue hot water bottle – someone who is down and in need of comfort.

House A person. A semi-detached house – someone happy with their partner. A detached house – a loner. A terraced house – a person who likes the company of others. A house with narrow windows – a person with a narrow outlook.

Housing estate A person (house) who is in a state about something. A council housing estate – a person who is in a state, and who is in need of counselling.

Hovel A person who does not take care of himself.

Humble pie Someone who is wrong, and needs to admit it and apologise.

Humpty Dumpty A person who has taken a fall and needs a pick-me-up.

Hurdle A situation you can overcome; it's up to you.

Hurricane A forceful person, someone who rips through life; someone you need to stand up to.

Hypnotist A person who likes to controls others.

I

Ice A current slippery, situation that involves the emotions and may get out of control – take care.

Ice-cream A problem that has to be licked in life, but it is not too difficult and the outcome will bring satisfaction.

Ice cube A person able to cool situations that are getting out of hand.

Ice berg A person to be wary of who is cold and unfeeling. What this person is showing on the surface does not reflect the depth of their thoughts or feelings.

Icon Somebody who has achieved greatness.

Identity bracelet Something you need to keep on hand to remind you never to lose your own identity.

Idol Someone who is revered but be aware that they may not be the person you think they are.

Igloo A person who on the outside may appear to be cold, but who has great inner warmth.

Imitation Someone who has little self-confidence and tends to follow another's lead.

Imp A person who is mischievous but who is loveable too.

Incinerator Someone who can reduce other's ideas and expectations to ashes.

Indenture An agreement between two people which can have lasting results.

Indicator Something that informs others which pathway you mean to take in life.

Industry There is a lot of work going into making a situation turn out well.

Infant A person who has a lot of growing up to do when it comes to handling life.

Inflammation An emotional situation that has flared up.

Injection A situation to which something has been added – or needs to needs to be added - in order to improve matters.

Ink There is a need to communicate.

Ink well You are allowing people to dip into your resources.

Inland Revenue Something is owed; it is now 'payback' time.

Intruder Someone is intruding in a situation where they have no business.

Invasion A situation in which someone is taking over, trying to gain control over it; your weakness is their strength.

Iris A situation where you should be looking into things more deeply.

Iron Something in life needs to be ironed out.

Ironing board A support to help the smoothing out of things. White ironing board – supporting the smoothing out of things using balanced thinking.

Island A person isolated from others. Lets life go on around them without getting involved.

Isolation A situation in which you feel you are all on your own.

Ivy Someone who clings to others and unable to support themselves.

J

Jack (for the car) A support for when you feel your body is letting you down. Listen to what your body is telling you.

Jacket The physical body.

Jackpot Something you have been striving for which, at the end of the day, has made everything worthwhile.

Jack Russell (dog) A man who keeps on about nothing.

Jade A person feeling under the weather.

Jagged A person or situation that needs to be straightened or smoothed, otherwise you could get hurt.

Jail A situation in which you feel hemmed in – you cannot see a way out.

Jar A person. The type of jar will give more detail. A jar of pickled onions – someone in a pickle.

Jasmine A person who is nice to be near who will climb high in life given enough support.

Jaundiced A person who needs to have a more positive outlook on life.

Jaw A person who likes to talk.

Jazz There is a need to jazz up your life; things are a little stale.

Jelly Someone nervous, cannot make up their mind.

Jellyfish Someone who gives the impression of being quite weak and ineffectual but who can sting you so much that it hurts.

Jester A person who should not be taken seriously in the present situation.

Jet (of water) A time when you feel overcome by the pressures that life has put upon you.

Jewel A person of great value or experience. A natural gift or talent.

Jigsaw A situation where things need to be fitted together.

Jockey A person who can handle power.

Jog A reminder to get started.

Joiner Someone who has the ability to keep the family together.

Journey An opportunity to learn and grow.

Judge Someone who is a good judge of people. Someone who is judgemental.

Jug A person – the type of jug illustrates the type of person.

Juggernaut A person who seems larger than life but who carries a heavy load.

Jumble sale A situation which has resulted in your life becoming a bit of a jumble. Get rid of what is not needed around you.

Jumper A person who jumps from one thing to another. A person whose life at present is unstable.

Junction You have reached a point where you need to choose in which direction you must go.

Jungle Life – we are all animals in the jungle of life.

Jury A group of people who together can have quite an effect either for good or bad.

K

Kaleidoscope A colourful person who is changeable.

Kangaroo A person who takes life in leaps and bounds.

Keep (castle) Someone well insulated against the onslaught of life's problems.

Keg A person small in stature but well contained.

Kennel A man who feels he is being left out of things in family matters.

Kettle A person who gets 'steamed up'. A situation that is 'on the boil' and should be watched in order to prevent it 'spilling over' and people getting hurt.

Key The answer to a situation. The type of key is important as it will indicate in what area the answer lies.

Kilt A man who skirts around things.

Kindergarten A person just beginning to learn from a lesson in life.

King (a king amongst men) A man to look up to.

Kiosk Someone who is confined to one avenue and has little chance of expanding to explore another.

Kipper A material situation that smells fishy.

Kiss A seal of approval.

Kissing Paying lip service.

Kitchen Preparation to be in service.

Kite Take off, get going. A high flier. A yellow kite – be positive and get going. A white kite – take off but keep your thoughts in balance, be level headed about it.

Kitten A female child, a girl.

Knave A male who is not to be trusted.

Knee A need to bend - more flexibility required when it comes to give and take.

Knife A situation that needs to be cut down to size.

Knife and fork Wisdom (in words) that is there for you to be taken in small pieces so that you fully digest (understand) it. One step at a time.

Knight A man who will bring release to someone in a dark period of their life.

Knitting needles   Something needs to be knitted together, to be put into order, when completed a pattern will emerge. Knitting needles with wooden handles – as above to do with a family situation. Knitting needles using brown wool – again as above but to do with a material situation.

Knock   There is a need to get your attention. Take care with a situation around you that it does not have a 'knock-on' effect.

Knot   A situation that needs to be tied up - or untied.

Knuckle   You need to knuckle down to something that is going on at present.

L

Label   Don't label everyone in the same way!

Laboratory   A situation that requires some careful research.

Labrador   A man who helps others to see their way along the pathway of life.

Labyrinth   A person whose life has become very complex.

Lace   A situation that requires a lot of delicate work to bring it all together.

Lace (shoe)   Something in connection with the direction you are taking needs to be tied up securely.

Lacquer (hair)   A situation about to arise that needs a firm hold. Putting a finishing touch to a situation ahead.

Ladder   The means to reach a higher level to cope with a situation.

Lake   This is a period of your life when things are now settling into a calm.

Lame   A situation in which you are unable to give your full support. You are restricted.

Lamp   A person who gives out light and comfort.

Lampshade   A protection for someone who is giving too much of themselves in life.

Landscape   Your outlook in life.

Lane   A way of thinking that is dark, dreary and narrow.

Lark (bird)   A person who does not take life seriously – larks about.

Lasso A situation needs to be held in order to prevent it getting out of hand.

Lawn A situation in your life that will need constant care and attention, sort it out and it will be to the advantage of yourself and others.

Lawn mower The means to bring a current situation (underfoot) under control.

Laurel wreath Achievement – an award for what has been won or overcome.

Lavender bush A person who soothes and relaxes you.

Leaf A member of the family.

Leak There is a need to give less of yourself to others because you are being drained by this.

Leap There is a situation in which you should take care before committing yourself – look before you leap.

Leather A person who wears well and copes well with the pace of life

Ledger A person who always tries to balance the material side of life with the spiritual.

Leech Somebody who clings and lives off others.

Leg A support through life.

Lemon A person who has been taken advantage of.

Letter A person bringing news.

Level A situation in which someone needs to 'level' with you, be straight.

Lick There is a problem which you need to overcome.

Lid There is a situation which you need to put the lid on for now.

Life boat A person who goes out to help others in their storms of life.

Lift Someone who is always able to lift others in the ups and downs of life.

Light Things need brightening up around you. There is a situation around you in which you need enlightenment.

Lighthouse A person who helps many in distress in the storms of life.

162

Lightning Enlightenment connected with the storm that you are going through in your life.

Lily (water) A woman able to keep afloat in life.

Limousine A person larger than life, but still comfortable to be with.

Line You have come as far as you can in the situation, now leave it. There is a need for you to 'toe the line'.

Link Things need to be brought together, linked with a current situation.

Lion A man who is a person of strength in the jungle of life.

Lioness A woman of determination who does everything for her family.

Lips Someone is being insolent (lippy). Red lipstick - speaking emotionally (be careful). Pink lipstick – keeping emotions in check.

Litter Be aware that there is a lot of rubbish going on around you that you need to brush aside.

Lock Something needs to be secured.

Locket You are keeping something personal close to your heart – open up!

Locust A person who seeks to destroy anyone who gets in their way.

Loft The mind.family.

Log Someone who is cut off, or has cut themselves off from their family.

Lollipop A problem that can be licked with perseverance.

Loot A situation where somebody is taking from others – be aware.

Lorry A worker.

Luggage You are carrying around a lot of things from your past which you need to sort out.

M

Mac (raincoat) Protection for an emotional time.

Magazine You, the person. Whatever the subject of the magazine is what you should be selling to yourself e.g. home alterations – you should be trying to alter yourself; make over – you should be altering your make-up, your character.

Maggot. A situation that is eating away at you or a person who is having the same effect on you.

Magician A magical person to have around.

Magnet A person who attracts and draws the attention of many.

Magnifying glass Able to see (understand) things to the smallest detail. Are you magnifying a situation? A person who enlarges on things in life – exaggerates.

A situation that needs to be examined more closely.

Magpie Very family orientated, loyal, constant and faithful.

Mangle A person or a situation where the emotions have been wrung out.

Mansion A dignified person.

Manuscript A situation in hand where the choice of words plays an important part.

Map A situation is mapped out for you. You have the choice of which way to go.

Marbles Someone not in control.

March Get on with it but keep in step with what is going on with the problem.

Marigold A person who can be both wise and positive and also in control.

Market There will be a variation of things coming on the market to help you.

Marquee A person who will give shelter to many for a short time.

Marrow Someone with an inflated ego who has little going for them.

Marshmallow A person who is too soft.

Mascot A person who stands out from others and who brings something special to the people around them.

Mask There is a need to mask your feelings. A person who is hiding their true self.

Match There is a need to lighten up a situation in the family.

Material A need to sort out a material (money) problem.

Matron A person who is quite at home being in charge of others.

Mattress Your foundation in life.

Maze You have a problem and need to find your way out of it.

Meadow Pastures green.

Meal Food for thought. A problem that you shouldn't blow up out of proportion (make a meal of).

Measure A situation in which someone is either unable - or needs to – measure up to things.

Mechanic (car) A healer, the car represents the physical body.

Medallion A situation where something of consequence has been achieved.

Media A situation where the means to communicate will be offered to you as an aid to sorting things out.

Medicine There is a situation where someone needs to have a taste of their own medicine!

Meditation There is a need to sit down quietly to think about something that is on your mind.

Medium A problem in which there is a need for someone to intercede in order to help.

Melon A strong, positive person who will nourish you with their wisdom.

Mercedes A strong person – the best.

Mermaid A female with a 'fishy' tale to tell.

Midwife A person who is there to help in a new venture.

Milk Mother or mother figure. Glass of milk – things will become clear regarding the mother figure. Milk churn – a situation to do with the mother figure which churns you up inside.

Mill Somebody going through the mill.

Minstrel A person who uses words to bring upliftment and leaves people feeling happier.

Mirror Reflection, thinking things out. Reflect, think back.

Mist A situation in which it is difficult to see which way to go.

Mole A person who is a loner and burrows their way through life. A person who works hard unnoticed.

Money Currency – power in the form of wisdom.
Paper money – less powerful because it doesn't last.

Monkey A person who is a mischief maker.

Monster A person who is unspiritual and not nice to know!

Moon A person who sheds light on your darkness.

Mop A means of clearing up an emotional situation.

Mosaic An intricate situation where things are brought together and the full picture emerges.

Mosque A person who has built up a great fund of spiritual knowledge – the spiritual you within (the inner temple).

Motor bike A powerful situation where you need to be in control and well balanced, take care.

Mould A situation has been left too long and should be settled.

Mountain A problem or experience that needs to be overcome. A mountain with one smooth side and one jagged side – a problem to be overcome where there is both an easy and a difficult way to do it.

Mouse A female who is timid and quiet but someone to be wary of. A mouse in a trap – a female who is trapped by her own deviousness.

Moustache A situation where you cannot see what is right under your nose.

Mouth organ Someone being used as an instrument for speech.

Move Something is now on the move; things will 'get going' for you.

Mud An unpleasant situation underfoot.

Mug A person who has been made a fool of.

Mule A person who carries a far too heavy load and is used by others. A person who can be very stubborn.

Mushroom Someone who has grown in the dark i.e. they have learned from unhappy or unpleasant experiences which constituted the dark times of their life.

Music Teaching that gives help and upliftment to others. Music sheet – the words to give upliftment.

Mustard A situation which has resulted in overheated emotions. Positive steps should be taken to cool things down.

Mutton Somebody who is not acting their age.

Muzzle A situation where you have not been allowed to say what you think. Think before you speak. There is a situation in which you should not get involved.

N

Nail There is a need for something to be secured.

Naked A situation in which something or someone will be exposed.

Napkin (baby's) A new event in which there is a need to cover up something private.

Nausea A person or a situation that leaves a nasty taste in your mouth - you are sick of it!

Navigator A person who is able to steer you through life.

Neck Support for a situation that is ahead of you.

Necklace Linked with something that what is going on around you. A necklace of coloured beads – surrounded by colourful people.

Needle Someone who cannot resist annoying (needling) others.

Neglect A person in need of tender, loving care.

Nest Someone who has worked hard to provide comfort for their family.

Nest egg A person who will provide in times of need.

Net A situation in which you are caught up.

Nettle Be careful how you handle a situation – you might get stung! There is a need to get on and deal with the situation (grasp the nettle).

Newsagent A giver of news.

Nib A situation in which there is a need to get to the point when communicating.

Night A situation in which you are being kept in the dark about something.

Nightdress A situation to do with a woman – at the end of the day it is necessary to put up with it (wear it).

Nightingale Someone who sings sweetly – tells the truth in a gentle way so that it is more acceptable and who sings in the dark i.e. brings help and comfort to those going through a dark period in their life.

Nightmare Something that needs to be brought out and discussed.

Nit A situation ahead in which there could be some 'nit picking'. Take care not to be involved.

Nod Someone is going to be in agreement with you – give you the 'okay'.

Nomad A non-materialistic person who is always 'on the move'.

Nose A situation that is right in front of you that does not smell right.

Nougat Something that will need a lot of thought (chewing it over) but keep your thoughts balanced.

Noughts and crosses Something that is going on between two people where there cannot be a compromise.

Novel Someone whose life has been full and interesting and from whom many lessons could be learned.

Nudge Someone needs to be prompted to get on with things.

Numbers Each number has a symbolic meaning. It is necessary for you to work out what it is in relation to yourself and your situation – it could be indicative of a period of time or a number of people etc.

Nurse A person who is caring and nurses people through their problems.

Nursemaid Someone who has to deal with childlike people.

Nut A person who is difficult to get to know – hard nut to crack – (the kind of nut is important).

Nutcracker A problem that would ordinarily be difficult to 'crack' will be overcome because you have the means – the tool – to do it.

Nutmeg A situation in life that needs to be spiced up.

O

Oak tree A person in the family who has grown to great heights and strength through life's experiences.

Oar An extra aid to help you make your way through a difficult situation in life that is going on at the moment.

Oasis A situation where you feel you have been deserted but there is no need to despair as help is on the way.

Ocean The sea of life. A person who is very deep – you can never get to the bottom of them.

Octopus A person who can't keep their hands to themselves. There is help coming your way (many hands make light work).

Oil A person who can inflame or calm – pour oil on troubled waters.

Ointment There will be help available to ease the pain that a current situation is causing you.

Onion Someone with many layers to their emotions.

Opening An opportunity that is coming. Something is going to open up for you. A new beginning.

Orange Wisdom – there is plenty within to be shared with many (the fruits of one's wisdom).

Orchid A very special person who should value themselves and not allow others to undervalue them, should not sell themselves cheap.

Ostrich Someone who buries their head in the sands of life – immerses themselves in their own affairs to avoid being involved in those of others.

Outlaw A person who chooses not to conform.

Ovation Success in meeting a challenge against great odds.

Overall A person who is conscientious in their work.

Overflow There is too much going on in your life; there is a need to ease up a little.

Owl A wise person.

P

Pace Give yourself a little more time with the current situation.

Pack Put away something that has been on your mind.

Paddle A means of helping yourself to get through life.

Page A part of your life (book of life).

Paint An indication that your outlook regarding the current situation will be freshened up; you will have a clearer and brighter perspective of things. (The colour of the paint is important.)

Palace A person who is regal and respected.

Pancake Feeling flat.

Pandora's box However bad the situation may seem, hang onto hope and you'll come through.

Pansy A cheerful person who is self-reliant.

Pantomime A situation in which there is no order.

Paper A situation that can easily be torn apart.

Parachute A situation in which things will open up for you to help you – have no fear; you will be protected from a fall.

Paradise The state of mind to which we all aspire.

Park You are in a situation where you can 'park' yourself and enjoy sharing your life with others.

Parliament A decision will be made that will govern your life in a more positive way.

Parrot A person constantly wanting to give of the word (talking). They can be quite vicious with their tongue; repeat a lot. A person who will repeat what you tell them so be careful what you say!

Parsnip A person who will make a point but with love – the sweetness of parsnip. They are one of the best (the cream).

Party A reason to celebrate. A celebration.

Passageway The passage of time.

Passenger You are taking someone along with you in life – do you need to?

Patch A situation in which there is a need for a 'get together' to sort it out (patch things up).

Path Life's pathway.

Patrol car A person who is caring and who protects others.

Pattern A situation where everything is in place and cannot be changed.

Pavement You will soon feel a little more safe and secure.

Pawnbroker's ticket A temporary situation that can be redeemed.

Pea Like-minded, like peas in a pod.

Peach A peach of a person – very kind and very loveable.

Peacock A very colourful male who gives the impression that he thinks a lot of himself.

Peak You have reached your goal and are at the height of your success.

Peanut A situation that is difficult to digest, chew it over well.

Pear A man (roughness of skin).

Pearl Wisdom obtained from the trials, tribulations and irritations of life. A string of pearls – access to a tremendous amount of wisdom. Pearl earring – wisdom will be acquired within a year to do with an ongoing situation.

Pebbles People in your life, often from the past (the sands of time).

Pedestrian Someone who walks through life; doesn't let things worry them.

Peer Somebody who has reached a position spiritually and is looked up to by others.

Peg Security – a reassurance that you will be secure despite the current material problem.

Pelican A comic on the surface but practical and self-sufficient underneath.

Pen There is a need to get in touch with someone.

Pencil A member of the family who is weak within.

Penguin A person who only sees things in black and white and can be cold emotionally.

Penny Something has just dawned on you (the penny has dropped).

Penthouse A person with pent up emotions.

Pepper pot A hot-tempered person.

Perfume The very essence of a person, good or bad.

Petticoat A situation where all is not revealed.

Pheasant Someone 'game for anything'.

Piano A person able to bring upliftment by communicating on a one-to-one basis or to an audience of many. Someone who is comfortable on their own or with many.

Pickles A situation where things are in a mess.

Picnic Something is going to be brought out into the open giving food for thought.

Pier A situation in which you are going to be given the opportunity to look at the turbulence of life from a safe distance.

Pig Someone who is content with their lot in life.

Pigeon A messenger.

Pillar Support for you in a current situation. You are well respected.

Pillow Support for ahead. A more restful time ahead.

Pilot This person will bring you down to earth with regard to an ongoing situation.

Pimple A small eruption of thoughts or feelings that may cause unrest.

Pin In connection with the material side of life indicating that things will be held together.

Pineapple Someone prickly and thick skinned.

Pine cone Someone who has 'dropped off the tree' – out of the family and is now regretful.

Pioneer A person prepared to go into the unknown not knowing what is ahead – a brave person.

Pip A person who irritates.

Pipe A warning to be careful what you say. Indian pipe – pipe of peace – speaking in peaceful terms.

Piranha A person who can devour verbally and emotionally.

Pirate A person who takes from others.

Pistol There is a potentially dangerous situation in your hands – take care.

Pit A situation to be aware of that can bring you down (depressed).

Pixie A person who is mischievous but not with malicious intention.

Planet A person or situation out of reach, unreal.

Plant A person – the type of plant is significant.

Plantation A place where many people have the opportunity to grow spiritually together.

Plastic A person who is insincere.

Plate A situation where something has been served up with very little effort having been put into it.

Plate full There is too much going on in your life.

Platform An experience or situation where you have had the chance to raise yourself in the eyes of others.

Pliers A situation where you will be able to get a strong grip on things.

Plough A situation you have to plough through before a decision is made.

Plug A need to stop wasting energy on someone else.

Plum A person who has had the best of things in life.

Pocket Personal and private, something to do with the material life.

Pogo stick In order to get ahead, you need to have your 'downs' as well as your 'ups'.

Poker An emotional situation that needs a fresh input.

Pole Something to hold onto, to use as a support. Greasy pole – an impossible task and for no purpose, a 'no win' situation.

Policeman A person able to keep order in a situation that is around at the moment. A need for some law and order in your life.

Policeman's helmet Something ahead in which you will need to be in charge (self discipline).

Polish Brighten up your life and put a shine on things.

Polony Someone angry and emotional.

Pomegranate A person who has not much to offer, red – may be quick to anger, there is much to discard about them and can be, much ado about nothing. It is hard work to find the goodness within them.

Pond A situation in life which is stagnant – no flow.

Poodle A pampered man who can be snappy.

Poppy Emotional memories of something or someone special.

Porcupine Someone who needs to be handled carefully – gets the needle.

Port Coming into a safe haven.

Porter A situation in which you may find yourself in which you are at everyone's beck and call, helping to carry their load (problems).

Postcard A situation where there is a need for a few words of advice, don't overdo it!

Potato (couch potato) Someone who just sits around and does nothing.

Powder puff Finishing touch to a situation in front of you.

Power point There is something available to give you extra strength (power).

Pram or pushchair Pushing ahead with a new beginning.

Pregnant Expectation of a new event.

Prescription You will be given the answer that will help you to heal within.

Prison A situation in which you feel trapped.

Programme Something that has been planned for the near future.

Prune A need to cut back.

Public house A person in service to many in different ways.

Puddle A small murky situation that is the aftermath of tears.

Puppet Someone who does not have a mind of their own – allows others to 'pull their strings'.

Puppy A boy or young man.

Purse A person – the contents of the purse are equivalent to the value of the person i.e. a full purse indicates that they have an abundance of power in the form of wisdom. A situation that is very personal. Worn, brown purse – giving money out on a regular basis – there is a need to stop!

Puzzle Something needs to be sorted out, putting the pieces together to get the full picture.

Pyjamas A current situation to do with a man. At the end of the day it is necessary to put up with it (wear it).

Pyramid A strong base on which to build enabling you to grow and reach a high point in your life.

Q

Quarry A hard stony situation that has opened up, you'll need strength to handle it.

Queen A woman who rules the roost.

Queue A situation that is going on and on but where your patience will be rewarded in the end.

Quilt Something that covers you in life. A patchwork quilt – each patch represents a different phase of your life and is an achievement of which to be proud.

R

Rabbit Someone who talks a lot – 'rabbits on'. White rabbit – a well balance person who speaks a lot, and whose words are sound.

Racing car A person who races through life and who needs to slow down and not be in such a hurry.

Radish Someone who gets 'hot under the collar' when dealing with people.

Raffle ticket A person prepared to take a chance –the luck of the draw.

Raft A person open to all elements in life emotionally and mentally. Needs to build a stronger shell around themselves.

Rain Tears.

Rainbow A storm in your life is now over and there is a pot of gold (wisdom) there for you if you have learned from the experience.

Raincoat A person who will be helped through an emotional time.

Rake To rake over your life, putting it to rights, discarding that which is of no good to you and levelling things up.

Rally A situation where you should be prepared to gather (rally) round.

Ram A nasty man – male rotter, take care.

Ransom You will be freed from a problem over which you have had no control.

Rash Something that is now out in the open for everyone to see.

Rat Someone (a male) who keeps gnawing away at you.

Rattle (baby's) There has been a new event that has gone unremarked but people will now sit up and take notice!

Razor blade The situation is going to be a lot smoother now.

Record It's the same old tune; change the record. Let bygones be bygones.

Red You are 'seeing red' (angry) you need to control your emotions.

Reflection Take a look at yourself – or another person around you – do you like what you are seeing?

Reindeer A female who can hurt with direct confrontation.

Removal van Something is now on the move; things will get going for you.

Rescue A feeling of release from a situation.

Rhinoceros Thick skinned, can be clumsy and insensitive to people's feelings.

Rhubarb A situation in which a lot of nonsense is being spoken. Sharp words are being spoken.

Ribbon Tying up something in readiness for what is ahead (the colour is important).

Rice A new start in life.

Rice pudding Things linked with your new start in life will not be so hard now.

Rigid You need to give a little, bend a little in a situation around you.

River Life, which until now has been controlled in one way or another, will now open up.

Robin A spiritual person who makes sacrifices for others.

Rock A person who gives you strong support.

Rock (a stick of) A sticky situation that emerges when it is unwrapped.

Rocking horse A situation where you are getting nowhere.

Roller skates A situation in which you need to get going.

Rook Someone who does not relate well to others, people do not feel comfortable with them – in fear of being 'rooked'.

Rose A person who is all heart (very kind). Red rose – love. White rose – the highest form of thank you for something that you have done for somebody. Yellow rose – a thank you for being positive in dealing with a situation.

Rose bush Someone very prickly. A rose bush that needs pruning - a prickly person who needs cutting down to size.

Rubber There is a need to remove a person or problem from your life.

Rugby ball Something you have in hand that you need to pass on.

Running There is a need to get away from a person or a situation.

S

Saccharine A person who is artificially sweet - their feelings are not genuine.

Sack A situation in which you will no longer be needed.

Safe There is a need for you to keep yourself private from others; you must not allow anyone to have the 'combination' to intrude on your thoughts and feelings.

Sailing ship You, the person, are about to set sail on the sea of life – you are on your way to a new adventure.

Sailor Someone who sails through life.

Salute A tribute to something you have achieved in the battle of life.

Salt The aftermath of tears.

Sand Time – the sands of time.

Sandals Your direction in life is opening up

Sauce (bottle) A person who can be cheeky.

Sausage A person (in a skin). A raw sausage – a person who is still hurting and emotional.

Saw Something that enables you to cut things (e.g. problems) down to size.

Scaffolding A situation or a person needing support and to be held together.

Scales Balance – someone needs to balance their way of thinking and get things into perspective in the current situation.

Scar An emotional situation that has been with you for too long; it is time for it to heal.

School A person who schools others to bring them up to standard in life.

Scissors Something that needs trimming down or someone who needs cutting down to size or even cutting out of your life.

Scooter (child's) A need for a balance between work and rest.

Scrapbook A person who holds onto things from the past and who needs to scrap some of the memories.

Screw A person who can twist in and out of a situation. Someone who is all 'screwed up' inside.

Scythe It's in your hands to cut out trivialities so that you can see where you are and where your priorities lie.

Sea Life.

Seagull A person who is gullible.

Seed The beginning of things to come.

Seesaw A situation between two people in which they are up one minute and down the next.

Settee A situation that two people are sitting on.

Sewing machine Getting your material life together. Helping to bring together something to help with a material problem.

Shave Once the problem has been removed, things will feel smoother.

Shed A person who is a loner in life.

Sheep Someone who is easily led by others or another.

Sheep dog A man who guides and brings others together.

Shelf A need to put a situation to one side for the moment – shelve it. Something that has been shelved should now be brought to light.

Shell A body without a spirit.

Sherry A toast to what has been achieved.

Shield A situation in front of you where you will be well protected, have no fear.

Ship A person. A canoe – someone paddling through life on their own. A life boat – someone who rescues people from the storms in their life. A liner – a people carrier, someone who carries a lot of people. A tug boat – someone who helps to bring people safely 'into port' i.e. guides people who are having a problem finding their way in life.

Shirt A man feeling annoyed about something – 'shirty'.

Shoes Your direction in life.No shoes – no direction. Tap shoes – somebody who is 'on tap' i.e. available when needed. Boots – direction to help in a working situation.

Shop Serving others.

Shower of rain A few tears, a little sadness that you have coped with.

Sideboard Something very personal that no one should be allowed to delve into.

Silver The highest form of spirituality.Silver tray – something that will be served up to you with the highest motive.

Skipping rope A help to keep in step with the situation.A skipping rope with wooden handles – as above to help you to handle a family situation.

Skirt Someone skirting around a situation.

Skull The framework for whatever is ahead.

Skylark Someone who aspires to the heights of whatever they do, but will help others on the upward pathway -- admired and well liked.

Slave A person whose life is controlled by others against their will.

Slide A problem in which things are going to get easier and you will soon have your feet back on firm ground.

Slippers A need for a rest from what is going on in life at the moment.

Slug A person who is the lowest of the low.

Smoke A hazard warning.

Smoke alarm A health warning – don't delay in taking action.

Snow A hazard, need to take care with conditions underfoot (what is happening at present). Look where you are going. Be careful.

Snowball Something that is thrown at people – cold words.

Snowdrop A person who has made their way through their hard and cold times. Someone who is highly spiritual and is able to come through all conditions intact.

Soap An ongoing situation of no value.

Socks Making your direction more comfortable to tread. Socks that need darning – someone who has to 'make do and mend' in their material life.

Soldier Someone with a fighting spirit (in an emotional war). Just soldier on.

Soot The residue of an emotional time – fire symbolising emotions, what is left when the emotions are burnt out.

Spade There is some spadework to be done. A new spade – preparation for your new life.

Spanner A tool i.e. a person who is instrumental in helping others in their daily struggles, helping them to loosen up or to tighten things up.

Sparrow A person who is a survivor in life – cheeky and chirpy, not letting life get them down.

Spinning top In a spin, not knowing if you are on your head or your heels.

Spectacles To get a better view.

Spice There is a need for more excitement in your life.

Spout There is a need for something to be said.

Sprout A young person who needs to keep their individuality while being part of a close-knit group.

Squeeze box A person who has been emotionally squeezed in life.

Squirrel A person who hoards things.

Staircase The means to tread step by step without rushing in order to reach whatever height to which you aspire.

Starling A young sociable female who likes to be one of a crowd.

Statue A situation in which there is no movement. A person who hasn't a lot of go in them.

Steamer A person who sails along in life under their own steam – takes things at a steady pace.

Steel Someone hard enough to take the knocks in life.

Step You are able now to take the first step with the opportunity to rise above the situation.

Stew A person who is 'in a stew'.

Sticky A situation which is unpleasant and embarrassing.

Sting A sudden hurt inflicted by another – be aware of the situation.

Stork A spiritual, well balanced person with great expectations.

Storm Bad conditions in life. Lightning storm – something coming to light during the storm.

Strawberry Someone who is loving and giving but who gets easily squashed and needs to toughen up. Strawberry jam – try to keep your emotions contained within yourself.

String You are being strung along in an emotional situation. A problem to which you feel you are tied – free yourself.

Submarine A person who could go down to the depths of despair but will always be able to surface again. A yellow submarine – a person who has a positive approach under all circumstances.

Suit A situation in which it is important to be businesslike.

Sun A person who gives out a lot of love, light and warmth.

Sunflower Seeking after enlightenment in a positive way. A person who gives out a lot of light and has the capacity to reach great heights.

Swallow Someone who needs to watch their words. Someone who needs to swallow their pride and not be so stubborn.

Swan A person who 'swans' along in life.

Swede A person who has been hardened by their life experiences but who will still do their best for others.

Sweet corn A positive person who enjoys being in service with others.

Sweets Taking in rubbish – junk, the difference between spiritual food and the psychic.

Swimming pool A pool of people all belonging to the same group – like minded.

Swing A situation in which you are getting nowhere, just swinging to and fro.

Synagogue A person who has built up a great fund of spiritual knowledge – the spiritual you within.

Syrup A sticky situation.

T

Table The base from which you serve to help others (type of table is important). Coffee table – aim to raise your service to a higher standard.

Tail A situation or story (tale) that you need to place behind you.

Tap (water) A need to have more control over how your life is running – it's in your hands.

Tattoo An experience that has affected you deeply and which has left its mark on you that is for all to see and difficult to remove

Tax (income) You are taxing your power – ease up.

Tea There is a need to take a break – relax more.

Teacher A person able to help you with your life because of what they have learned from their own experience of life.

Team Like-minded people who can work together.

Teapot A person who needs to speak out, to spout off about something. Always take care with how you handle it. Brown teapot – someone who needs to speak out about a material matter. Silver teapot – someone who needs to speak out in a spiritual way.

Teddy bear Something from your past that you still cling on to; it's time to place it aside.

Teeth There is something to chew over, to get your teeth into. Teeth that have been taken out – someone could be extracting (words) something from you – be sure that you are consenting to this. Teeth cleaning – a need for something to be polished up regarding something that is to be said. False teeth – there is a need to get a grip on the situation.

Telephone Communication. Telephone kiosk – a person who communicates well with others.

Television Receiver – communicator, giving the full picture.

Temple A person who has built up a great fund of spiritual knowledge – the spiritual you within.

Tent A person in a temporary situation – no need to worry.

Thimble Protection for something on hand, linked with a current situation.

Throat Control of what you say. Red scarf around the throat – a need to be in control of your emotions when speaking.

Thunder Someone or something in your life is creating a lot of noise.

Tie A situation involving a man where everything will be tied up in front (in the future). A gold tiepin – using wisdom to keep things in place for the future.

Tiger A woman who wants to get her claws in – not a nice person.

Toast (bread) Words of congratulation in respect of something that has been achieved.

Toe There is a need to 'toe the line'. Big toe – there is a *great* need to 'toe the line'!

Toilet Relief is at hand in the current situation.

Tomato An emotional female.

Toothbrush Cleaning something up in connection with something that is spoken.

Torch Something in hand to light the way. Someone in love (carries a torch for another).

Tortoise Someone who takes their time but gets there in the end.

Towel Something to absorb conditions that you are going through. A brown towel – as above to do with a material situation.

Tower A person who is a tower of strength.

Track A situation in which you are not allowed to stray – keep 'on track'.

Traffic lights A situation that is being controlled – the colour is important.

Trainers Linked with your direction in life in which there is a need of training.

Treasure Someone of great value.

Treasure hunt Hunting for something of value in life.

Tree In connection with the family.

Tricycle A person pushing ahead by their own efforts but who has extra support to keep them well balanced.

Trifle A problem that has been built up out of all proportion but is of no importance.

Tripe Someone is giving you a load of rubbish.

Trousers Someone (male or female) who needs to be more assertive (should wear the trousers more).

Trout (rainbow) A person who is very colourful and in the swim of things in life.

Trowel It is in your hands to achieve and you'll do it little by little.

Trumpet Someone who is boastful.

Tug boat A person who helps to bring others safely in from the storms of life.

Tulip Your mouth (two lips) – what you say. The colour relates to the way it is being handled.

Tunnel A dark period in your life that you are going through at the moment; look out for the light, it's coming!

Turnip Someone who has the potential to be balanced within.

Tweezers Something in front of you (future) is going to be put into shape to help you.

Twig A young member of the family.

Typewriter Words at your fingertips.

Tyre Something to support you, to help you on your way. A flat tyre – someone who is feeling flat because they are not getting anywhere.

U

Umbrella Needing protection from the traumas of life e.g. heated words, rain (tears), heavy storms

Undercoat There is some preparation work to be done before you can proceed with your plan.

Underlay Something to make the going easier in connection with a current situ (underfoot).

Undertaker Someone who will take the burden of ending a situation – putting it to rest.

Uniform There is a need to conform in relation to the current situation.

Union A group of people who work together for the same ends.

University The lessons of life.

V

Vacation There is a need to take a rest from the situation – leave it to others.

Vaccine There is a situation around you where 'prevention is better than cure'.

Vacuum flask A person who does not get affected by conditions around them.

Valley A low period in your life.

Vanguard Someone who is preparing the way for others to follow.

Vase A person (the type of vase is important).

Vegetable A person – the type of vegetable relates to the type of person.

Vehicle A person – the type of vehicle is important. Bus – a person who carries a lot of people.

Veil An emotional situation that needs to be hidden from others.

Velvet A material situation that will be smoothed out.

Vessel A person (the type of vessel is relevant and reflects the kind of person they are).

Violet A person who is shy and keeps in the background while thinking and acting in a caring way.

Violin A person well in tune with life who could be a leader.

Violin case A person who carries something valuable within. A wooden violin case – a member of the family who carries something valuable within.

Volcano An emotional eruption with damaging results.

Vulture A person who lets others do the work and takes their choice of the pickings.

W

Walking stick You will be given support in the situation.

Wall There is something stopping you going further with a situation – you're up against it.

Wand A wish for a change.

Wardrobe To do with the material life (holds material).

Warehouse A person who is spiritually aware.

Washbasin A surface problem to be dealt with.

Washing Cleaning up a material problem.

Washing machine A person who is feeling 'all washed out', is back and forth, continually 'in a spin'.

Wasp A cunning person who can sting you and get away with it.

Watch Something on hand that you need to watch (be careful).

Water Life.

Watering can Someone who is able to give a little help in life as a pick-me-up.

Waterfall An emotional situation where things have got out of control – the higher the waterfall, the bigger the situation.

Water lily A person able to stay afloat in life.

Waves A disturbance in life (making waves).

Weasel A person who is always able to talk themselves out of a situation or problem.

Weather The conditions that surround a person at the time.

Weaver Somebody who is helping to weave something together to help with a material problem.

Web Something that is being spun in which to catch you (deceit).

Wedding The ending of one kind of life and the beginning of another. A change of circumstances.

Weed A problem or person that needs to be taken out of your life.

Weighing scales A situation which needs to be brought into balance.

Well Something to be drawn on to help you through life.

Wheel That which goes around, comes around – wait and see.

Whirlpool A person or situation that is pulling you down in life.

Wig Something ahead that is false but can be changed.

Windmill Someone with the ability to sort the wheat from the chaff.

Window View of life.Narrow window – narrow view on life. Picture window – seeing the full picture.

Wine Enriched life.

Wings Something to give you a lift and help you to rise above things - you will soon feel better.

Winter A cold situation.

Wolf A man who is not to be trusted.

Wood The family – roots.

Woodpecker A family member who wears you down by peck, peck, pecking.

Worm A person who will worm themselves in or out of a situation.

Wreck A person who has been through the storms of life.

Wrench Adjusting to a situation.

Wringer Someone who has been or is going through a difficult emotional period.

Y

Yacht A person able to 'go with the flow' in life, handling conditions that present themselves.

Yarn Someone who tends to exaggerate but is very entertaining.

Yeast Something will help you to rise to the occasion.

Yellow Positive.

Yellow hammer A positive person who is a little 'ham-fisted' in their dealings with others. Because they have such a positive outlook on life themselves, they cannot understand other people's negativity. They can be insensitive, lacking understanding although they mean well.

Yucca A person who thrives in warm and friendly conditions but is very resilient and their balanced attitude to life and others will help them to grow regardless of the lack of encouragement.

Z

Zebra Someone who sees things in black and white.

Zip Keep your thoughts to yourself (keep your mouth zipped).

Zither A sensitive person who is highly strung.

Zombie A person who feels life has no meaning any more; feels dead emotionally.